Helping Staff Develop in Schools

Education at SAGE

SAGE is a leading international publisher of journals, books, and electronic media for academic, educational, and professional markets.

Our education publishing includes:

- accessible and comprehensive texts for aspiring education professionals and practitioners looking to further their careers through continuing professional development

- inspirational advice and guidance for the classroom

- authoritative state of the art reference from the leading authors in the field

Find out more at: **www.sagepub.co.uk/education**

Helping Staff Develop
in Schools

Sara Bubb and Peter Earley

Los Angeles | London | New Delhi
Singapore | Washington DC

WITHDRAWN

BOWLING GREEN STATE
UNIVERSITY LIBRARIES

SAGE Publications Ltd
1 Oliver's Yard
55 City Road
London EC1Y 1SP

SAGE Publications Inc.
2455 Teller Road
Thousand Oaks, California 91320

SAGE Publications India Pvt Ltd
B 1/I 1 Mohan Cooperative Industrial Area
Mathura Road
New Delhi 110 044

SAGE Publications Asia-Pacific Pte Ltd
33 Pekin Street #02-01
Far East Square
Singapore 048763

Library of Congress Control Number 2009930847

British Library Cataloguing in Publication data

A catalogue record for this book is available from the British Library

ISBN 978-1-84920-025-7
ISBN 978-1-84920-026-4 (pbk)

Typeset by C&M Digitals (P) Ltd, Chennai, India
Printed in Great Britain by CPI Antony Rowe, Chippenham, Wiltshire
Printed on paper from sustainable resources

Mixed Sources
Product group from well-managed
forests and other controlled sources
www.fsc.org Cert no. SGS-COC-2953
© 1996 Forest Stewardship Council

Contents

List of figures

List of tables

Acknowledgements

This book has been written to help staff develop in schools. As such, we would like to thank all the people whom we have spoken to as part of our research, particularly on the *Staff Development Outcomes Study* and *From self-evaluation to school improvement* as well as those we meet on courses at the Institute of Education. These people have been an inspiration to us in writing what we hope is a very practical book.

The folk at Sage are wonderful, so particular thanks must go to Jude Bowen and Amy Jarrold as well as the marvellous Jeanette Graham and all involved in the production of this book.

Most of all, we must thank our families and friends – especially Paul, Julian, Miranda and Oliver – for their encouragement and tolerance.

The authors are grateful to all those who granted permission for material to be reproduced in this book including: the CfBT Education Trust, Training and Development Agency for Schools (TDA), especially Chris Brown, CPD Leader, Teachers TV (all Teachers TV material was correct and available at the time of going to press), Human Resource Development Quarterly, Office of Manpower Economics, Teachernet, South Yorkshire LEA, Professor Chris Day and Professor Thomas Guskey.

Preface

Great staff make great schools. The organisations that make most impact on their pupils are the ones that choose their staff carefully and help them develop so that they are very effective, highly motivated and feel fulfilled in their work. By 'staff' we don't just mean teachers. In many schools, teachers are less than half of the total workforce. So we need to think about the development of everybody, whatever their role, so that as a group they can make a fantastic difference to children and their communities.

The last decade or so has seen a growing recognition in schools and colleges that people matter and that attention must be given to their needs, especially those concerning their professional and personal growth. Staff development is a field in which there is growing interest because people see it as such a vital part of school improvement, raising pupil achievement and enhancing their wellbeing. We hope that this book will help people think more deeply about the development and training of staff – all staff – in schools and other organisations. It is related to our second edition of *Leading and Managing Continuing Professional Development*, which might be a valuable source for those wanting greater detail than provided here. But in this book we have tried to be concise, practical and useful so that it will lead to even stronger staff development practice. This is vital, particularly in the current climate of schools having more responsibility for their own people, and indeed working with other schools in staff development clusters and networks.

Perhaps the most important developments in recent years have been the growth of the wider children's workforce and integration of a broader range of people into staff development systems. To be successful, we should know what individuals need, have plenty of ideas of how to help them progress and know that the impact of activities really does make a difference so that they can be even more effective in contributing to pupils' achievement and well-being.

We hope that this book will help improve human resource development and its management and leadership so that more people get a better deal and that their development is given the attention it merits.

In writing this book we have tried to do two things. First, we have summarised the most recent relevant research – some of which we have been personally involved in – to highlight the issues and current state of affairs. This gives a firm foundation for leaders and co-ordinators leading and managing staff development. Secondly, we have given examples and case studies of good practice drawn from a wide range of schools.

It is important to remember that development cannot be forced and that staff who are excited and motivated by the experience of their own learning are likely to communicate that excitement to pupils. Throughout the book, we draw upon the latest research and examples of good practice, where possible giving case studies and pen portraits.

Although our focus is predominantly on schools, staff development has to be well led and managed at three levels: that of the school, the local authority and at a national level. The key goal of all educational organisations is student learning, whereas the ongoing learning of teachers, support staff and other employees is not always prioritised or adequately resourced. Creating a culture of learning is crucial and this is shaped essentially by the attitude and approach of school leaders and governors towards staff development. There is a need to ensure that personal development is not marginalised – it is crucial to individual effectiveness and thus to the success of the school and young people. Schools need to achieve a healthy complementarity between system and individual needs. People matter and this has recently been recognised with the national training and development programmes for the leaders of staff development.

Structure of the book

The book consists of ten chapters and is divided into two parts: Leading Staff Development and Making Staff Development Count. We begin by looking at the leadership of staff development and its management (Chapter 2), before considering why staff development needs to be strategic and what that means. We often hear the claim that there is simply no time for staff development, so in Chapter 4 we look at ways in which time can be found for workforce development. The five development days (commonly called INSET days) are the focus of Chapter 5 and we investigate how we can make the most of this time.

The focus of the second part of the book is on the training and development cycle and how to get the maximum impact from your staff development resources. We begin with the area of impact evaluation and stress how important it is to plan for impact right at the outset. Needs identification is the focus of Chapter 7 where we consider procedures for identifying teachers' and support staff's needs. We argue in the following chapter for the need to personalise learning and consider what we know about how adults learn. Chapter 9 is concerned with the all important area of meeting needs and it considers the range of activities that are available to develop people, such as coaching-mentoring, observation and the growing world of e-communities. In the final chapter we outline useful publications and resources which we feel will be helpful to you.

Throughout the book we share what we know by drawing upon research, often our own, and providing examples of good practice. We address the practical considerations and management and leadership implications to help you develop your strategy for developing the school workforce: so that they and the organisation are learning-centred.

Sara Bubb and Peter Earley,
Institute of Education,
University of London

About the authors

Sara Bubb

With an international reputation in the induction of new teachers and staff development, Sara speaks at conferences and runs courses throughout the country and abroad. She is England's Advanced Skills Teacher (AST) network leader and has featured on and been a consultant for many Teachers TV programmes. She sits on the Training and Development Agency's (TDA) *Professional Teacher* editorial board and its Research Advisory Group. Sara has worked as an academic at the Institute of Education since 1995, leading research projects such as *The Sinnott Fellowships: the impact of the outward facing school*, the *Staff Development Outcomes Study* and *From Self-evaluation to School Improvement*. She was the consultant for Chartered London Teacher status from 2005 to 2008. For six years she has been the new teacher expert at the *Times Educational Supplement*, writing a weekly column and answering questions on its website. Sara is an assessor of advanced skills, excellent, overseas-trained and graduate teachers and higher level teaching assistants and has inspected 25 schools. She has written many books, papers and articles.

Peter Earley

Peter is a professor of leadership and management at the London Centre for Leadership in Learning at the Institute of Education, University of London. Formerly a school teacher and further education lecturer, on returning to England after a five-year spell teaching in an Australian university, he became a full-time researcher at the National Foundation for Educational Research. It was during this time that he worked on several projects on school leadership, including the well known study on newly appointed secondary headteachers (Weindling and Earley, 1987). His central research interest has remained leadership and leadership development. Recent research projects include studies of fast-track or accelerated leadership development programmes and the evaluation of the pilot of the National Professional Qualification for Headship.

Sara and Peter have worked together on several projects including the role of professional development in high performing schools and the evaluation of the *Future Leaders* programme. Both have published widely in the field of school leadership, school evaluation and professional development and their co-authored books and reports include: *Leading and Managing Continuing Professional Development* (2nd edition, 2007, Sage); *Managing Teacher Workload: Work-life balance and wellbeing* (2004, Sage); *From self-evaluation to school improvement: The role of effective professional development* (2008, CfBT); *Staff Development Outcomes Study* (2008, TDA); and *What do we know about school workforce development? A summary of findings from recent TDA-funded research projects* (2009, TDA).

Abbreviations

AST	Advanced skills teacher
BETT	British Educational Training and Technology Show
CA	Classroom assistant
CIPD	Chartered Institute of Personnel Development
CPD	Continuing professional development
DCSF	Department for Children, Schools and Families
EAL	English as an additional language
EPD	Early professional development
GTC	General Teaching Council
GTCE	General Teaching Council of England
GTCS	General Teaching Council of Scotland
GTP	Graduate Teacher Programme
HEI	Higher education institution
HLTA	Higher level teaching assistant
HMI	Her Majesty's Inspectorate
HoD	Head of department
ICT	Information and communications technology
IEP	Individual education plan
INSET	Inservice education and training
ISCTIP	Independent Schools Council Teacher Induction Panel
ITT	Initial Teacher Training
LA	Local authority
MFL	Modern foreign languages
MPS	Main pay scale

MTL	Masters in Teaching and Learning
NAPTA	National Association of Professional Teaching Assistants
NCLSCS	National College for Leadership of Schools and Children's Services
NOS	National Occupational Standards
NQT	Newly qualified teacher
NVQ	National Vocational Qualifications
Ofsted	Office for Standards in Education
OTT	Overseas-trained teacher
OTTP	Overseas-trained teacher programme
PGCE	Postgraduate certificate in education
PLC	Professional learning community
PM	Performance management
PPA	Planning, preparation and assessment
QTS	Qualified teacher status
SDP	School development plan
SEF	Self-evaluation form
SEN	Special educational needs
SENCO	Special educational needs co-ordinator
SIP	School improvement plan
SLT	Senior leadership team
SMT	Senior management team
SSAT	Specialist Schools and Academies Trust
SSSNB	School Support Staff Negotiating Body
STRB	School Teachers' Review Body
TA	Teaching assistant
TDA	Training and Development Agency for Schools
TES	*Times Educational Supplement*
TSN	Teacher Support Network

1

Why staff development matters

> **This chapter covers:**
> - **What is staff development?**
> - **Staff development makes a crucial difference**

What is staff development?

Staff development matters. But what exactly do we mean by that? Here are some definitions:

> Continuing professional development (CPD) consists of reflective activity designed to improve an individual's attributes, knowledge, understanding and skills. It supports individual needs and improves professional practice. (www.tda.gov.uk/cpd)

> Continuing professional development: ongoing training and education throughout a career to improve the skills and knowledge used to perform a job or succession of jobs. (www.bnet.com/cpd BNET Business Dictionary, 2009)

> CPD is a combination of approaches, ideas and techniques that will help you manage your own learning and growth. The focus of CPD is firmly on results – the benefits that professional development can bring you in the real world. (www.cipd.co.uk/cpd)

We don't favour the use of the terms 'CPD' or 'continuing professional development' in this book because we think that many colleagues in the school and college community may feel excluded by the term 'professional'. That's a term usually associated with teachers. We feel strongly that the development of the whole workforce is vital, not just the teachers who in many schools make up less than half of the total staff. So, except when citing others, we try not to use the term.

Even if the word 'professional' were omitted we would still consider the above definitions fairly narrow. For us, staff development is:

> an ongoing process encompassing all formal and informal learning experiences that enable all staff in schools, individually and with others, to think about what they are doing, enhance their knowledge and skills and improve ways of working so that pupil learning and well-being are enhanced as a result. It should achieve a balance between individual, group, school and national needs; encourage a commitment to professional and personal growth; and increase resilience, self-confidence, job satisfaction and enthusiasm for working with children and colleagues. (Bubb and Earley, 2007, p. 4)

Or, put more simply, staff development is about adult learning, ultimately for the purpose of enhancing the quality of education of children and young people. That's why it's so important.

Let's unpack what we mean.

1. Staff development is an ongoing process

   The process is what is important: development is something that is within the person all the time, not something done to or provided for them.

2. It encompasses all formal and informal learning experiences

   We develop in many ways: through the planned and formal activities as well as the learning through experience, to say nothing of the thoughts that occur while watching a film or which pop into your head in the shower.

3. It enables all staff in schools, individually and with others, to think about what they are doing

   Thinking about what you're doing is crucial. As Socrates said,

   I cannot teach anybody anything, I can only make them think.

4. It enhances knowledge and skills

   You've got plenty of knowledge and skills and now you're going to get yet more. We're not into deficit models.

5. It improves ways of working so that pupil learning and well-being is enhanced

   The goal of all development should be that ultimately things are better for the children and young people.

6. It achieves a balance between individual, group, school and national needs

   We need to develop and help others to so that the benefits are multiplied.

7. It encourages a commitment to growth

   As Benjamin Britten said, 'Learning is like rowing against the tide. Once you stop doing it, you drift back'.

8. It increases resilience, self-confidence and job satisfaction

   Working with children and young people can be tough, especially on the emotions, so we need to look after and develop our resilience, confidence – and enjoyment of our work.

9. It gives staff renewed enthusiasm for working with children and with colleagues

Staff development makes a crucial difference

In this book we draw upon recent research projects we have been involved in to illustrate key points about the effective leadership and management of staff development. Our recent research for the Training and Development Agency for Schools (TDA) examined the relationship between staff development outcomes and school performance (Bubb et al., 2009). Did staff development make any difference to how pupils performed? Yes, it did.

Staff development makes a crucial difference. It ultimately leads to school improvement whether couched in terms of better teaching and learning, or student and staff welfare and well-being. People development is more effective in enhancing the performance of organisations, including schools and colleges, than any other factor. We believe that it:

- helps everyone be more effective in their jobs, so pupils learn and behave better and achieve higher standards
- improves recruitment because:
  - a school or college that is focused on staff development will be looking to find people with the right skills
  - word gets around about the places where you are looked after, and where you are not
- contributes to a positive ethos where people feel valued and highly motivated
- makes for a learning-centred community – the pupils are learning and so are the staff
- is a responsibility and an entitlement
- improves staff retention because staff feel fulfilled and successful
- saves money – the costs of recruiting and inducting staff are high.

Organisations which give serious attention to the development of their staff will reap rewards: effective staff development enhances students' learning and well-being because the adults improve their ways of working. Staff development should also add something to the organisation's overall capacity to improve; and it should be able to build upon the collective learning of its people. As a result of the training and development opportunities made available staff will benefit in many ways. For example, perhaps they will have:

- thought more deeply about what they are doing
- enhanced their knowledge
- developed skills
- improved ways of working
- shown a greater commitment to professional and personal growth
- become more resilient
- gained greater self-confidence
- increased job satisfaction
- shown more enthusiasm for working with children
- shown more enthusiasm for working with colleagues
- increased a colleague's learning
- enhanced a colleague's well-being
- enhanced student and pupil well-being
- increased student and pupil learning; and
- increased other staffs' learning in order to improve things for their students and pupils.

All this as a result of effective development of the organisation's workforce? We believe so!

Ideas about the central importance of staff development to the success of any organisation are not new. For example, the Chartered Institute of Personnel and Development (CIPD) see people as the prime resource of the organisation, claiming that managers get better results (in terms of productivity, customer satisfaction, profitability and employee retention) by managing and developing people better. In education, the James Report, published as long ago as 1972, (DES, 1972) stressed that each school should regard the continued training of its teachers – we would now say 'workforce' – as an essential part of its task for which all members of staff share responsibility. This government report ensured that the further professional development of staff became a national issue and it still is today for the simple reason that people development is crucial for school improvement. The staff is the most important resource of the organisation, but particularly in people-based organisations like schools and colleges.

As the bulk of a school or college's budget is spent on paying staff it is also crucially important to get the most out of your people to improve pupil well-being and learning. The professional and personal growth of all staff is a key component of developing children's and young people's learning. The ongoing development of staff is crucial in helping to address the organisation's priorities identified to bring about improvement, enhance the quality of the learning experience, and generally make things better for pupils. In *The Logical chain* Ofsted (2006) found that 'schools which had designed their CPD effectively and integrated it with their improvement plans found that teaching and learning improved and standards rose' (p2). Overall, staff development was found to be most effective in the schools where the senior managers fully understood the connections between each link in the chain (what we prefer to call the staff development cycle) and recognised its potential for raising standards and enhancing well-being and therefore gave it a central role in planning for improvement.

Recent research findings show that the school workforce consider training and development of great importance. For eight in ten teachers, staff development is an important factor when considering both their future in their current school and in the teaching profession (NFER, 2008). The *State of the Nation* (McCormick et al., 2008) study identified a number of reasons for teachers choosing to undertake training and development, namely to:

- work with other colleagues
- improve their professional abilities
- address immediate school needs
- gain more information
- have a positive impact on pupil learning
- improve academic achievement
- follow-up previous development activities
- address immediate classroom needs
- gain a better understanding of national curriculum requirements.

A growing number of schools are making a particular point of developing support staff, often because they have been neglected in the past. They constitute a growing proportion of the staff and have been shown to have a significant role to play in children's learning. For instance, in one primary school we researched, teaching assistants (TAs) were catered for specifically with training aimed at the learning styles of particular staff members and to fit in with their shorter working hours.

At many schools, people have progressed significantly in their careers as a result of their development: they've gained qualifications and moved to more highly skilled posts. For instance, a midday supervisor became an ICT technician and then a qualified teacher.

> *I started here as a TA, having been out of work for a while. As a result of working here, I went to college to get my NVQ2 and now I'm really into education – I'm passionate about it. More knowledge: more power! After my NVQ3 the natural progression was to HLTA. Then I did the Assessor course to assess TAs at level 2 and 3. Now I am doing a course to train assessors how to assess. I am also halfway through an English degree. It's a massive thing for the students because I am a great example of teaching life skills and resilience.*

At one school we researched there was a particularly strong emphasis on developing staff for leadership roles and promoting them just before they were ready as a way to stimulate them. This school personalised its career development approach, providing flexible working and responsibilities for people caring for both young and elderly dependents.

The effects of training and development on staff – both teachers and support staff – can be significant. Its impact can change people's lives and careers as can be seen in the following activity.

 Activity: Watch *CPD – evidence of impact*
www.teachers.tv/video/31815

Take a look at this programme and hear about the impact training and development in one school has had on three members of staff: the school nurse, a TA and a PE teacher.

And of course it can make people happier in their job. One school keeper was reinvigorated by being asked to take over the school gardens and this became a huge learning journey of finding out more about plants and resulted in him running a thriving gardening club. When staff feel valued they go the extra mile.

PART A

LEADING STAFF DEVELOPMENT

2

How to lead staff development

> **This chapter covers:**
>
> - **What does staff development leadership look like?**
> - **What's involved in leading and managing staff development?**
> - **Sharing the load**
> - **Keeping informed**

What does staff development leadership look like?

Staff development doesn't just happen. Although individuals have a responsibility for their own development, the school too needs to be learning centred and provide opportunities for all staff to continue their learning. Staff development therefore has to be led, co-ordinated and managed well to make a difference. What does strong staff development leadership look like? Table 2.1 shows the features of schools where it's working well and where it isn't.

In researching outstanding schools we found that leaders of the schools with the strongest staff development engendered an ethos in which all pupils, teachers and support staff were valued and seen as learners in their own right. Indeed several head-teachers said that adult learning was instrumental to their schools' continued improvement and was a key part of their shared vision and values. In one school a newly qualified teacher explained that staff development fitted in with the school's vision statement (which she could quote verbatim!) about valuing and developing everyone.

Leaders fostered, and staff felt, a sense of both entitlement to and responsibility for their own development and learning. Individuals were motivated to identify and seize opportunities, and showed initiative in doing so. Staff felt valued and many went the extra mile as a result. There were numerous examples of high motivation levels and impressive commitment, such as a site manager who had worked at the school for 35 years and loved his job so much that he started work at 3am rather than the contracted 6am.

Several very successful staff development leaders started by being responsible for new teacher induction and trainee teachers and then assumed responsibility for the

Table 2.1   Features of strong and weak staff development leadership and management (Bubb et al., 2009, p18)

Where staff development is well led	Where staff development is not well led
It is seen as a very important job.	It is tacked on to many other jobs.
The role is taken by deputy or assistant heads (secondary schools) or heads and deputies (primary and special schools).	The role is taken on by someone with too much else to do.
People have been leading staff development for a long time.	People are new to the role.
They have many years' experience not only in teaching but also in leadership roles.	People have limited leadership experience.
Leaders are well informed, know where to find out more and share their knowledge.	Leaders don't know what they don't know.
Leaders distribute responsibilities appropriately, including to senior support staff.	Leaders try to do too much themselves.
Staff development has significant investment in both time and money.	Staff development is poorly invested in. Staff feel constrained by the school's tight budget.
Administration is efficient and things run smoothly.	Admin systems are not efficient.
Staff development is strategic and focused on benefits to pupils and school improvement.	Staff development is not strategic and given to those who ask rather than according to need.
Governors are involved at a strategic level.	Governors simply attend training themselves but are not involved in a strategic way.
Staff development is closely linked with school self-evaluation and improvement plans.	Staff development is not closely linked with school improvement plans. Individuals are doing their own thing but not contributing to strategically planned improvement.
Investment in people's development appears to reduce staff absence rates.	High staff absence rates.

whole school workforce. This graduated responsibility, starting at the all important beginning of careers, seems a key to success.

Where staff development leadership was weak, people were relatively new to the role and some were new to leadership more generally. They had many other roles and so devoted little time to staff development, tending to perceive the role more in terms of co-ordination rather than leadership. They mainly had little administrative support and tried to do too much themselves. In several cases, the current postholder had taken over with varying degrees of willingness from someone who had been ineffective or absent on long term sick leave.

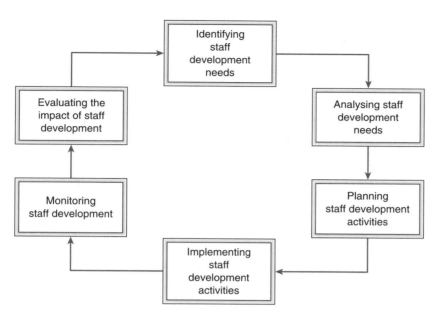

Figure 2.1   The staff development cycle

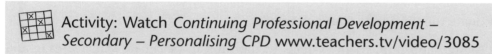

Activity: Watch *Continuing Professional Development – Secondary – Personalising CPD* www.teachers.tv/video/3085

This programme looks in more detail at how staff development is led and tailored to the needs of all staff:

- Through classroom observation
- By developing skills to meet individual targets
- By encouraging individual action planning
- By reviewing recently promoted posts
- By listening to student feedback.

What's involved in leading and managing staff development?

Leading and managing staff development well requires an enormous amount of work. An understanding of the staff development cycle (see Figure 2.1) is vital. You need to identify and analyse institutional and individual needs, plan how to meet them, meet them, monitor progress and then evaluate the impact on staff and pupils before starting to look at new needs. Although impact evaluation is the final part of the cycle, as we argue in Chapter 3, it is very helpful if questions about evaluation are raised at the outset in order to ask the question, what do we hope to achieve?

Staff development leaders need to have an overview of every stage of the cycle to ensure that key tasks are done and done well. Here's a list for starters:

1. Identify and analyse staff development needs:

   - organise systems that identify training and development needs in the context of the school development plan

- identify individuals' needs, or set up systems for others to do so
- factor in national or local policy initiatives that affect specific groups of staff.

2. Plan how to meet needs:

- plan how best to meet these needs within a budget and based on up-to-date knowledge of the options available and accreditation
- create a staff development plan, demonstrating how the school will provide the necessary opportunities that have the desired impact.

3. Arrange for training and development to take place, matching the needs of individuals and groups of staff to appropriate activities:

- support, monitor and assess NQTs according to the induction guidance
- support, monitor and assess trainee teachers and other staff who are on placements, e.g. nursery nurses
- induct new staff into how the school as a whole works, as well as their roles
- find the funding and allocate resources in line with priorities and monitor resource expenditure on staff development
- help design and co-ordinate training programmes and development days
- support and advise others in their staff development role.

4. Evaluate the impact on staff and pupils:

- design and implement systems to monitor and evaluate staff learning and performance
- evaluate and improve the school's training and development.

Thus, you can appreciate that the leadership and management skills required might include:

1. Strategic planning – to see the bigger picture and understand whole school needs

2. Facilitation – to help lead a learning-centred community

3. Administrative and organising skills

4. Coaching – to encourage

5. Emotional intelligence – to understand people's needs and aspirations and respond to them

6. Financial – making the most of the budget

7. Communication – orally and in writing

8. Evaluation – to measure impact

9. Technical – computing, databases, websites

10. Passion – for lifelong learning.

Job description

Job descriptions will vary. Here is an example of one:

Staff development leader job description (adapted from Dudley LA)

The key task of the staff development leader will be to ensure the efficient and effective delivery of the school's staff development policy. With the induction and development of the school community a central element in the raising of standards, improving quality and facilitating recruitment and retention, the role is a significant one and likely to be undertaken by a senior member of staff. The main responsibility for staff development lies with the individual with the leader acting in a supportive and facilitative role.

Purpose

1. To oversee and manage the school's staff development processes in accordance with the staff development and Performance Management policies.

2. To ensure the process assists colleagues in developing their practices and enriches the quality of the educational provision of the whole school community.

3. To sustain motivation and continuous learning amongst the whole school community, encouraging an ethos of lifelong learning.

Responsibilities

1. Manage a staff development strategy that ensures all involved in the school community have access to high quality induction and continuing support and development.

2. Organise and carry out an effective auditing and identification of the school's needs and those of the school community and advising colleagues on the effective identification of their own needs ensuring that they have opportunities to clarify their needs through Performance Management and appraisal.

3. Produce a staff training plan to submit to the headteacher and Governing Body including advice on budgetary implications.

4. Organise a range of types of quality provision which is based on 'Best Value' principles, is personalised to the needs of individuals, allows the school community to develop skills and competencies progressively especially those identified in the appropriate standards framework.

5. Communicate and update opportunities to appropriate staff development colleagues.

6. Provide opportunities for staff development within the school including supporting and advising others in their roles and through organising whole school development days, in collaboratives and partnerships and through external provision.

7. Maintain effective links with key providers, agencies and organisations such as the LA, TDA, DCSF, GTC, NCSL, SSAT, subject associations, dioceses, faith organisations and commercial providers.

8. Produce appropriate monitoring records about individual and whole school staff development uptake and resource expenditure.

9. Receive feedback from participants and liaise with providers about relevant follow up.

(Continued)

> *(Continued)*
>
> 10. Organise and administer a reliable and explicit evaluation of the quality and impact of staff development activities.
>
> 11. Organise effective dissemination of good and successful practice to ensure that such practice is embedded and reinforced.
>
> 12. Facilitate the accreditation of the staff development activities undertaken by individuals.
>
> 13. Advise and contribute to the obtaining of appropriate quality standards in organisations that support effective staff development, e.g. Investors in People.
>
> 14. Report as necessary on staff development issues to the leadership team and Governing Body including advising on the benefits of participation in relevant initiatives and projects.
>
> 15. Receive training and support as appropriate in order to fulfil this role effectively and attend useful providers' sessions.

What should a staff development policy contain?

A staff development policy could include:

- a definition of what staff development is and what it aims to do

- who it is for

- roles and responsibilities

- processes, procedures and practice

- evaluating the impact of staff development

- links to other policies, e.g. induction, staffing and pay

- how staff development relates to school improvement and performance management

- annual staff development plan including the five development days.

The policy should ensure individuals are aware of each other's roles and responsibilities and the support and development opportunities open to them.

Self-evaluation

You might want to audit or evaluate staff development provision as a whole or for a specific group such as NQTs or new TAs. These questions could be helpful prompts:

What is available for this staff category within the school, locally and nationally?

What has been provided recently?

What were the outcomes of this provision?

What are the identified needs of this category of staff for the forthcoming period?

What provision should be made to meet these needs?

Table 2.2   The diagnostic framework for staff development leadership, London's Learning (www.lgfl.net/lgfl/sections/cpd/londonslearning/ede/). Specific thanks go to London's Learning for their permission to include Table 2.2. *London's Learning* represents the experience of over 60 school and local authority CPD leaders from 25 London boroughs. The resource is written and edited by Vivienne Porritt at the London Centre for Leadership in Learning, Institute of Education.

Emerging	Developing	Establishing
There is a growing recognition of the need to support professional development of all staff to achieve school priorities.	There is a shared aim to build capacity to develop all staff with established plans to achieve this.	There is a clearly stated and shared vision for the school as a professional learning community to which all members of the community contribute and from which they will benefit at all stages of their career.
A CPD policy is in place which highlights training opportunities.	CPD policy links to performance management, team plans and school improvement plans.	CPD policy emphasises that CPD is key to self-evaluation, standards of teaching and learning, and school improvement.
The CPD co-ordinator reports to the school Leadership Team. The Job Profile focuses on operational management of professional development. There is a recognition that the role needs to become more strategic.	The CPD co-ordinator is a member of the school leadership team with other major responsibilities. Within the Job Profile the CPD co-ordinator has an overview of the learning of all staff in the school.	The CPD leader is a member of the school leadership team whose overall responsibility, as stated in the Job Profile, is for the learning of all staff in the school and its impact on standards and school improvement.
Training opportunities are managed by a CPD co-ordinator.	Career and professional development of staff is supported by the CPD co-ordinator.	Career and professional development of staff is supported by leaders at all levels and the CPD leader is responsible for a whole school approach.
Some team leaders see it as their responsibility to support teachers' learning plans.	All team leaders have delegated responsibilities to support individual learning programmes and to evaluate the quality of provision. Some team leaders have been trained in coaching and mentoring skills.	All team leaders are responsible for their team's learning programmes; ensure that individual learning plans impact on teaching and learning; inform performance management targets; contribute to school self-evaluation and impact on school improvement priorities. Team leaders have been formally trained in the skills of coaching and mentoring.
A CPD summary, as currently required, is in the Governors' annual report to parents.	The headteacher reports regularly to governors on CPD opportunities, evaluation of quality of provision and value for money.	A nominated governor promotes the learning of all staff; ensures that resources are appropriately allocated; evaluates the impact of the school's professional development framework on learning and teaching and disseminates findings to the governing body.

Does this group of staff have access to training and development which are adequate and appropriate to their circumstances?

Are there any issues and concerns about the provision for this category of staff?

Frameworks such as the one in Table 2.2 can help in self-evaluation: knowing where your leadership of staff development is and where you'd like it to develop.

Sharing the load

There's a lot to the role: as well as leadership, there is also a great deal of management and administration so it must be more than one person's job. A range of other people can and should be involved in supporting and co-ordinating staff development. One person, usually a member of the Senior Leadership Team, needs to have a strategic overview of how staff development can make a positive difference to the school or college and how this can be achieved. Then a range of different people will have varying roles:

- Governors have a strategic role in overseeing staff development
- Team leaders have a responsibility for their team's development
- Performance reviewers identify people's strengths and development needs
- Other staff such as advanced skills and excellent teachers, higher level teaching assistants (HLTA), school business managers, mentors and coaches can support colleagues' development.

And of course all staff have a personal responsibility to develop their knowledge and skills.

Table 2.3 shows the advantages of different leadership and management structures and ways in which they can best be made to work.

Table 2.3 Staff development leadership and management structures (Adapted from www.cpdleader.com, doc 2g. Developed by Tim Lomas (Lincs SIS) for the East Midlands CPD Partnership)

Structure	Advantage	Disadvantage	To work well, it needs
A single staff development leader	Coherence Expertise	Workload Isolation Difficult to be expert in whole workforce Succession problems	Maximising expectations on individuals and teams Leader has status in the school Adequate time for the role
Several staff development leaders	Sharing of workload Expertise for different groups Sharing of ideas Sustainable More ownership	Diluted expertise Can lack big picture Co-ordination takes time	Needs an overall co-ordinator/leader Clear responsibilities and expectations Monitoring systems to ensure equity
Staff development leader for a network	Economy of scale when planning provision Dedicated expertise – possibly a full-time role Can draw on a much greater range of talent Awareness of a greater range of contexts	Energy dispersed Overwhelming role Ensuring equity Leader remote Managing different contexts and cultures Co-ordination takes time	CPD leadership teams across the network Need for clear structures and systems Consensus on budgets, development days, etc.
No overall staff development leader	Everyone can have a sense of ownership and responsibility Can be fair if budget is divided equally amongst all staff	No responsibility No strategy or coherence No targeting Recycling of ignorance The most aware and those who shout loudest gain the greatest benefit Not responsive to new initiatives	Needs co-ordination Clear requirements and structures for all the workforce Need to link with SEF and school improvement planning

Table 2.4   Staff development job titles

Words	Staff group	Roles
CPD	Teachers	Co-ordinator
INSET	NQTs	Leader
Human Resources	Trainee Teachers	Manager
Professional Development	Support Staff	Officer
Staff Development	Teaching Assistants	Administrator
Professional Learning	Admin	Head
	Site	Deputy
		Assistant head
		SENCO

We know from research (Robinson et al., 2008) that in secondary schools, staff development is usually led by a deputy or assistant headteacher. In primary and special schools the headteacher has the most significant leadership role, albeit distributing leadership or delegating tasks. Job titles have a combination of the words in Table 2.4. These are indicative of the complexity of the role – and how much is expected from it.

Perhaps some new terms would help raise the profile of and give clarity to the role of staff development leadership. What do you think of these?

- STADle – the staff training, appraisal and development leader

- STADco – the staff training, appraisal and development co-ordinator

- STADman – the staff training, appraisal and development manager

We use the word 'staff' rather than 'professional' to emphasise that we're looking at the whole school workforce not just the teachers. The other key words are 'training', 'appraisal' and 'development' – what is the difference between them? You could have versions for those who have a staff development leadership role with different groups of the workforce, such as OfTADle – the office staff training, appraisal and development leader. The names might be different but the people fulfilling them must be clear as to their leadership responsibilities. It is important that, 'The title chosen should signal the cultural and strategic vision for CPD as well as indicating the purpose and actions of those holding the role' (Porritt, 2008, p22).

Different models

Distributing the leadership and management of staff development is vital for success – and your sanity. But how do you do it? It's useful to look at some different models. In one special school, for instance:

- the headteacher saw herself as leading staff development

- the two deputies led staff development in the senior and junior sections of the school

- the head's PA kept track of paperwork and booked courses, speakers and liaised with people

- the bursar kept track of spending

- the bursar led staff development for admin, kitchen and site staff

- teachers were seen as leading the development of their team of support staff

- the lead TA led TA induction, trained people in safe handling and had been on high level coaching courses (intended for heads and deputies) so that she could coach and counsel others

- a retired teacher trained staff on risk assessments

- one TA trained staff on how to use different hoists for moving disabled pupils

- another TA shared his specialist knowledge about sophisticated technology

- another TA rolled out training in Makaton throughout the school

- the AST trained staff in this and other schools on the latest techniques for teaching pupils with visual disabilities.

This extensive training of each other was part of people's jobs, and done well and willingly.

In some schools, staff development is led by someone with a non-teaching background. One school appointed a professional development manager, with experience of mentoring but not teaching. Another school's full-time Training School and CPD Manager has a background in project management rather than teaching. He successfully manages the training school budget and organises the professional development of all staff, from the bespoke to whole school training. He's very good at keeping track of who's done what and offers a menu of professional development activities that take account of money, time and resources. He is part of the senior management team.

In another secondary school, the development of the 70 support staff is managed by the headteacher's personal assistant. She ensures that induction and Performance Management (PM) are rigorous (not just a paper exercise) through training PM reviewers. She encourages people to do formal qualifications such as NVQs so that there is recognition that they've moved forward. Her impact is great. For instance, even though the school does not have any more HLTA posts, four people are applying for HLTA status because it seems exciting and a way to raise their status. One of the four had previously been a very negative person, which the school thinks shows that PM and staff development have made a difference. She is so successful that she has become leader of the local support staff training hub.

The senior midday supervisor of one primary school organises training for lunch time, breakfast club and after school club staff and has written a handy booklet. This is particularly useful for new staff as it summarises all they need to know. She is immensely proud of her achievements and role. Training covers first aid, manual handling, playground games and behaviour. She's organised wet play boxes and set up colouring competitions with prizes. She's introduced a reward system at lunch time to give incentives to children. All this has had a powerful impact because children are readier for learning in the afternoon if happy at lunch time. She is also mentoring the new family worker who as a result has had much training in the four months since starting the role (e.g. child protection, sex education, transitions) all of which have enabled her to get up to speed rapidly.

Keeping informed

The staff development leader role also requires a great deal of knowledge and keeping up to date in a rapidly changing world. There are training programmes such as the National College's Leadership Pathways unit on the Strategic Leadership of CPD and the TDA's national development programme for staff development leaders, both of which contain distance learning components. The following journals and websites are very useful for staff development leaders in aiding them with their role. Many of them have e-newsletters which are a quick way to see the latest developments. There are further publications detailed in Chapter 10.

- The TDA's CPD zone www.tda.gov.uk/cpd is a certain boon with an ever increasing number of resources and a directory of training opportunities. There is an *e-directory for CPD leaders* with links to resources that are openly accessible through websites.

- Periodicals, such as *CPD Update* www.teachingexpertise.com and *Professional Development Today* www.teachingtimes.com/professional-development-today are very handy.

- The GTC's network www.gtce.org.uk/ also has some useful documents and events.

- *Everybody's learning* www.cpdleader.com has been produced collaboratively by a collection of experts and practitioners across the nine LAs in the East Midlands, so it combines up to date knowledge with pragmatic ideas of what will work.

- *London's Learning* www.lgfl.net/lgfl/sections/cpd/londonslearning contains examples of practice and documents in Word and PowerPoint from practitioners across the capital for people to easily customise.

- The *International Professional Development Association* www.ipda.org.uk is an organisation for all who are interested in professional learning and development. They have a website and hold conferences. *Professional Development in Education* www.tandf.co.uk/journals/ is its academic journal with four issues a year.

Other sites are of great use for keeping up to date with the latest developments, especially in educational research. Again, we recommend signing up for email alerts where possible.

The *Teacher Training Resource Bank* (TTRB) www.ttrb.ac.uk

This provides access to the research and evidence base informing teacher education. All materials are quality assured through a rigorous process of academic scrutiny and monitoring. It enables searching of resources and provides personal support via an e-librarian.

The Research Informed Practice Site www.standards.dcsf.gov.uk/research

This site provides a searchable database of summaries of research written for practitioners. It offers a range of facilities including the ability to send digests to a friend option.

Research for Teachers www.gtce.org.uk/teachers/rft

The GTC's Research for Teachers (RfT) appraises research studies and presents case studies to illustrate the findings.

National Teacher Research Panel www.standards.dcsf.gov.uk/ntrp

This website provides resources for practitioners interested in undertaking research in their own schools and classrooms. These include summaries of practitioner research and guidelines for using research for development.

Educational Evidence Portal www.eep.ac.uk

This portal brings together research and evidence for educational and children's services.

National Education Network www.nen.gov.uk

This includes a large-scale online swap shop, the National Digital Resource Bank, giving access to resources designed and tested by teachers.

Teachernet http://www.teachernet.gov.uk/docbank/index.cfm?id=13558

The Teachernet website has Research Bites, Which are 90-second PowerPoint presentations with summaries of key research for practitioners to share among colleagues and at staff meetings. They focus on practical classroom issues.

Keeping up to date and being aware of what's coming up (environmental scanning) is part of being strategic and it is this aspect of leading staff development that we next consider.

How to be strategic

This chapter covers:

- Why staff development needs to be strategic
- What do you mean by strategic?
- How to be strategic

Why staff development needs to be strategic

Staff development has to meet a variety of needs: individual, team and organisational. There are also needs resulting from local and central government policy initiatives. Unsurprisingly sometimes there will be tensions between these various types of need within a school or college and decisions will need to be made about how they will be met. Staff development leaders have to ensure that any training and development will meet the needs of both individuals and organisational priorities. They need to ask:

National needs

- Is the school preparing for the current changing educational scene?
- What is the evidence base that ensures that the school is developing with regard to the Every Child Matters outcomes?
- Is the school developing its extended provision appropriately?
- How do we know the needs related to addressing new skills and qualifications frameworks?

Institutional needs

- What are the main sources of evidence for the school's current needs?
- Is there a sense of whole institutional ownership of the self-evaluation form and school improvement plan?
- Does the school improvement plan look at success/maintenance issues as well as identified gaps and weaknesses?
- Is the data analysis robust and fully understood by the workforce?
- Is the evidence gathered at different levels, including by the pupils themselves?
- How do individuals, teams, governors, parents and the community contribute in a genuine and constructive way?

Individual needs

- Are the needs and aspirations of staff members being looked at in the round?

- Is performance management working?

- How far does the school address pastoral and career needs?

- Is there an issue of the reliability of individual needs information or is it a case of people not knowing what they don't know (something that can result when systems are too formulaic and mechanistic)? (Adapted from CfBT/Lincs, 2007.)

Resources are not infinite. This is why staff development needs to be strategic.

What do you mean by strategic?

Leaders of staff development need to be strategic: that is to be forward thinking, trying to foresee what lies ahead and which influences may be important in the future. Strategic thinking involves rising above the day-to-day operational issues and looking at the bigger picture. Strategic leaders, including those of staff development, involve themselves in five key activities:

- direction setting

- translating strategy into action

- aligning the people and the organisation to the strategy

- determining effective intervention points

- developing strategic capabilities (Davies and Davies, 2009, p15).

Strategic leadership of staff development is about providing for the sustainability of the school. It builds capacity and capability to meet future challenges as well as those of the day-to-day. It means schools must become 'learning communities'. Being strategic in your leadership means making decisions and integrating staff development with school improvement plans so that teaching and learning improve and standards rise. You need a medium to long term plan of how you're going to move closer to your school's aim and vision by helping individuals develop. A strategic approach:

- puts pupil learning at the heart of all staff development

- aqligns school, team and individual staff priorities

- uses pupil data to inform decisions about staff development

- makes efficient use of resources.

Here are two examples of where staff development and its leadership were not strategic:

> School A:
>
> Training was mainly given to those who asked rather than according to need or to aid the journey towards some specific school improvement. The link between development

activities and pupil outcomes was not clear to all staff. Some people were more invested in than others, and this caused resentment. The over-invested staff felt overwhelmed and that they had been out of the classroom too much. Others in the school had their requests for training turned down. All this seemed to have been done without a clear strategy.

School B:

Much was spent on staff development but because it was not thought through or strategic it did not give value. In fact, some resources were wasted. For instance, people could think of no impact resulting from expensive international trips. For INSET days, the headteacher booked the teachers and all the support staff into a hotel for two days' training at enormous expense but nobody could think of anything they got out of it other than a vague notion of team building.

How to be strategic

Staff development needs to be closely linked with school self-evaluation and improvement plans. Done well, the process that leads to the completion of the school self-evaluation form (SEF) should:

- encourage a greater thoroughness and wide-ranging evaluation of the school's work
- provide a better understanding of evaluation
- involve more people in evaluation
- give greater attention to the views of stakeholders (Bubb and Earley, 2008, p10).

Individuals need to be aware of the link between their targets and the school development plan (SDP) and improvement priorities, as this example illustrates:

The SDP was a very democratic document: it arises substantially from the thoughts and discussions that subject co-ordinators have with their colleagues which, according to one teacher, gives the staff 'real ownership' of the plan. The SDP emerges 'from the ground floor up'. The SDP takes the holistic, physical shape of a large mind-map and was prominently displayed in the school for staff, pupils, parents and visitors to see. For each cluster of priorities they identify, there was a staff development branch. (Bubb et al., 2009, p20)

To ensure that the journey from self-evaluation to improvement is made as quickly and as well as possible, staff development has to be strategic. We identified ten factors that are important in using the outcomes of self-evaluation accurately to identify staff development needs and then meet them so that the school improves.

1. The leadership and management of staff development need to be effective.

2. People need a clear shared understanding of staff development.

3. The school needs to develop a learning-centred culture.

4. Individuals' development should be linked to the analysis of needs through performance management and career development as well as self-evaluation and school improvement.

5. The goal, and the reasons for it, must be clear and ultimately should make a difference to pupils.

6. The quickest, most effective and best value for money forms of staff development should be chosen based on what will suit individuals.

7. Staff development that involves discussing, coaching, mentoring, observing and developing others is highly effective.

8. Time needs to be made for staff development.

9. Staff development should be monitored and its impact needs to be evaluated.

10. Learning and development should be shared, acknowledged and celebrated for improvement to be sustained (Bubb and Earley, 2008, p27).

 Activity: Watch *CPD Leaders – Leading School-based CPD* www.teachers.tv/video/28595

How do the staff development leaders help staff work on their own development tasks as well as improve their school as a whole?

How are they being strategic?

Who to invest in

The challenge for leaders is to ensure that all sections of the school workforce get the development that will 'move them on'. In any size school this is difficult, but in a large one there will be more people to liaise with. Do you ask people what they want or wait for them to ask? You will find yourself torn between government and local initiatives, where the school wants to go and team and individual needs.

One way to look at what staff need and whom to invest in, is to use the performance and attitude to improvement grid (Figure 3.1). Use the horizontal and vertical axis to look at how well someone is doing their job and how keen they are to improve. You may see four broad categories of staff:

A. Someone who is doing their job well but doesn't want to improve needs motivation.

B. Someone who is doing their job well and wants to improve probably doesn't need training so much as resources, such as time, to enable them to develop.

C. Someone who is not doing their job well and doesn't want to improve probably needs a new job, either in the same school or somewhere else.

D. Someone who is not doing their job well and wants to improve is an ideal person to invest in as training is likely to help them do their job better.

Spending most time and money on people in Group D, who are not doing their job very effectively but who want to improve, is likely to have the most impact on whole school improvement. This is one of the reasons why new staff are worth investing in.

Who can help?

It's important to choose the best people to help you develop other staff. Advanced skills teachers (ASTs) are a powerful force for school improvement by developing others.

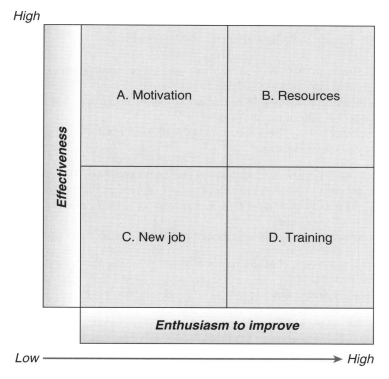

High

Effectiveness

A. Motivation	B. Resources
C. New job	D. Training

Enthusiasm to improve

Low ⟶ High

Figure 3.1   The performance and attitude to improvement grid (based on Glaser's Performance Analysis Grid, 2002, p4)

Although only 1 per cent of teachers in England have the status, they have a significant impact not only in the classroom but because, for one day a week, they share practice with other staff and schools. Since July 1998, 8,215 people have been awarded AST status. Government statistics show that in January 2008 4,300 ASTs were working in the role – 2,770 in secondary, 1,300 in primary and 220 in special schools. However, this number looks set to increase as government and local authorities appreciate their value in school improvement. Some headteachers strategically employ a number so that they can work together. At one secondary school a group of ASTs have initiated a cross subject peer observation and coaching scheme with teachers across the school.

Winning hearts and minds at the outset is a crucial factor in school improvement initiatives. This involves convincing the staff concerned, that the proposed change is (a) desirable and (b) possible. This can be done by sharing information and data, encouraging individual accountability, getting the right people involved and raising morale. Sometimes having 'ordinary' staff leading initiatives can have a greater influence than using the more usual leaders.

Case studies

The case studies below show how staff development and school improvement were integrated in a strategic way. We have identified learning points that might be useful for you to consider.

Case study 3.1: Improving mathematics

What they wanted to achieve: To have secured observable improvements in practice in all classes in the teaching of mathematics which, by the end of the year, would have translated into better performance by pupils, demonstrated in tests and internal school monitoring.

> Learning point: There was a goal but it was a little woolly. How much did they want to improve?

Why? The school was identified by the LA as coasting. There were poor value added results in all the core subjects, and no reason for this. An inspection was due and the LA predicted that it might move into a category, possibly requiring special measures.

> Learning point: There was a clear and urgent reason for action.

How? The strategy that the new headteacher devised included sharing the data at the first INSET/Development day of the year showing that the school was underachieving and what this would mean when inspected.

> Learning point: the new headteacher gave a clear evidence-based big picture of the underachievement of pupils, which won staff hearts and minds.

She then developed staff through lesson observation, modelling good practice, learning walks and work scrutiny.

a. Lesson observation and performance review

Employing criteria derived from the Ofsted inspection framework, each teacher completed before the observation an initial self-evaluation of teaching and learning in mathematics using the four-point scale. Most rated themselves at point three on the scale (satisfactory).

> Learning point: Self-review preceded observation of all staff teaching mathematics, which meant that individuals gained familiarity with how lessons would be judged.

In the first two weeks of the term the new head observed every teacher's mathematics lesson, which in most cases coincided with the teachers' self-evaluation. The head gave individual feedback, which identified strengths and areas for development. The observations pinpointed weaknesses across the board in mental/oral mathematics, challenge for able pupils, pace of lessons and passive learning. These were virtually identical to the weaknesses identified in the last Ofsted inspection some years before.

> Learning point: Lesson observation, to a consistent schedule and completed early in the term, was important in giving the head a secure basis of evidence from which to indicate areas for improvement. The teachers were unused to getting developmental commentary on their work and welcomed the feedback.

b. Modelling

During the first half of the term all the teachers, in pairs, observed the head teaching a daily mathematics lesson. Each visit was followed by a debriefing session.

> Learning point: The head was walking the talk. Observation in pairs with an agreed focus allowed comparison of impressions and judgements and debriefing sessions encouraged talk about teaching and learning.

c. Learning walks

These took place in two stages. In the first stage the head visited every classroom over two mornings, with a focus on observing active and independent learning in mathematics among the pupils. The head fed back her impressions to each teacher and 'published' on the staffroom notice board her overall findings, along with what had been agreed would be the next steps. In the second stage, each teacher undertook a learning walk in the same way as the head, gave feedback and presented their findings and next steps on the staff notice board. By the end of the term, every teacher had visited every other teacher's classroom, engaged in discussion and committed ideas to paper. The head felt this was an essential strategy for developing in every member of staff a sense of the 'bigger picture' of how the school worked.

Learning point: Staff were gaining a whole school perspective while picking up ideas from seeing other practice.

d. Work scrutiny

The senior leadership team looked at work in mathematics by selected pupils in each class. The focus was on the quality of the teachers' written responses, particularly the clarity with which they indicated the next steps for learning. The main findings were shared at a staff meeting.

Learning point: Impact was evaluated through work scrutiny and observations. Main findings and progress were reported frankly and to promote discussion.

Did it work? Yes, there were significant improvements in the Key Stage 1 results taking the school above the national comparative data for the first time in three years. There were similar results in Key Stage 2 in Maths and Science. Staff felt that they had learned a lot and developed professionally, saying, for example, 'Assessment now focuses more on the next steps that need to be taken'.

(Based on Bubb and Earley, 2008, pp40–41)

 ## Case study 3.2: Modern foreign languages

What they wanted to achieve: To start teaching French in a primary school so that after two years pupils would be achieving highly:

- *Year 4* – 80 per cent at level 2 for listening and speaking, 60 per cent for reading and writing; and 30 per cent at level 3 for listening and speaking, 15 per cent for reading and writing.
- *Year 6* – 100 per cent at level 2 for listening and speaking, 80 per cent for reading and writing; 65 per cent at level 3 for listening and speaking, 50 per cent for reading and writing; and 15 per cent at level 4.

Learning point: There was a clear long term goal related to ambitious pupil achievement.

Why? It was decided to start teaching French not only in response to the national strategy of teaching modern foreign languages (MFL) in primary

(Continued)

(Continued)

schools but also to fit in with the overall mission of this multicultural school which was to raise pupils' achievements, enrich their experiences and encourage positive attitudes towards the diversity of language and culture.

Learning point: They knew exactly what they wanted to achieve and why.

How? The initiative was led by the MFL co-ordinator with the support of the headteacher. She has only been teaching two years so needed to feel confident in her new role and have a clear understanding of the issues and her responsibilities. So she spent time at weekends and holidays looking at resources, meeting with specialists, visiting specialist centres and exhibitions and in term time attended a course for MFL leaders. This gave her a strong support group as well as greater knowledge, understanding and skills. She drew up a carefully considered detailed staged plan with the headteacher for the implementation of French.

Learning point: Leadership was distributed and time was invested in the new leader's development. She got up to speed quickly, choosing development activities that were very effective and minimised disruption to her class teaching.

Staff felt anxious about teaching French so a key aim was to ensure that high staff morale was quickly established. At the first staff meeting all teachers and teaching assistants completed an online assessment of their French skills and their level of confidence.

Learning point: The online assessment felt private to staff but meant that results could be seen quickly. Auditing staff skills and confidence gave a clear baseline from which they could plan.

As a result, it was decided to make use of the native French speaking teaching assistant.

Learning point: Using the skills of their own staff (rather than an outside expert) raised the status of the teaching assistant in question and all support staff.

At the second meeting the co-ordinator introduced the French schemes of work and good practice principles of teaching MFL.

Learning point: The selection of a structured scheme and lesson framework inspired confidence and made people feel that the initiative was taken seriously. People felt enthusiastic as a result of the co-ordinator's training, which was the first she had ever led.

The third training session for all staff took place at the National Centre for Languages with a Primary Language Specialist.

Learning point: Drawing on external expertise and a specialist venue inspired staff. High quality training at different levels met a range of needs.

This was followed by a social event.

Learning point: Continuously finding ways to create positive attitudes to ensure that French was a success was fundamental to the strategy.

As well as high quality training in and outside school there were:

- French themes for staff parties
- a Year 6 day trip to France
- a series of assemblies to promote knowledge about France

- the 'Vive la France!' whole school event to learn more about the country
- French songs incorporated into the weekly singing practice sessions.

Learning point: Staff and pupils were becoming immersed in the new language and culture and having fun.

The French lessons were planned and led by the headteacher or the MFL co-ordinator with the teachers in Key Stage 2 classes and carried on by the native French-speaking teaching assistant as he grew in confidence. A successful routine for each lesson was established.

Learning point: Teachers were not burdened straight away with planning and teaching French but built their confidence by joining in with lessons led by either the headteacher, MFL co-ordinator or teaching assistant.

At half-term some staff visited their linked school in French-speaking Canada. Two teaching assistants and three teachers gained external funding for this.

Learning point: The trip was motivating, rewarding and inspiring. The integration of support staff with teachers increased the team spirit.

Did it work? Yes, the MFL leader and the staff gained in confidence and, as a result, pupils made good progress. After just one term, the school was visited by inspectors as part of a HMI review of MFL in primary schools. The report said:

Pupils have made good progress in speaking and listening in the short time they have been learning French. They show positive attitudes to the new language and are keen to show off what they can already say. Planning and teaching are good and the leadership and management of the subject are outstanding. Very careful thought has been given to the development and sustainability of this new curriculum area.

(Based on Bubb and Earley, 2008, pp49–50)

Operating strategically also involves using time to good effect and it is to how time is found for staff development that we now turn.

How to find time

> **This chapter covers:**
>
> - **What we know**
> - **Ideas for finding time**
> - **Using existing time well**
> - **Blue skies thinking**

Finding time for staff development is a universal problem. This chapter looks at workable ways in which the development of the school workforce can be enabled by finding time for training and development.

Conditions of service are different for school teachers and support staff. The former, for example, are required to work for 190 days per year with an additional five days being used at the headteacher's discretion, usually for staff development, when the pupils are off site. There is no requirement for school teachers to 'clock up' a certain number of hours as is the case in many other professions, including lecturers in the Learning and Skills or Further Education sector (30 hours a year), and teachers in other countries. For instance, teachers in Hong Kong are expected to undertake 150 hours of professional development over three years, but this is a soft target and no auditing takes place.

In England, some schools expect staff to do a certain number of twilight training sessions in lieu of development days. However, specifying this number has resulted in people not doing more – seeing it as a quota to meet. There is a general expectation that teachers, as professionals, will need to keep themselves up to date with recent developments as well as wishing to improve their practice. The time needed to do this can be taken from the working year when the pupils may or may not be present (an entitlement) but also from other time too (a responsibility) outside of the official contracted hours. We argue at the end of this chapter that these arrangements are no longer working well and that there is a need to 'remodel' the teachers' year in order to better accommodate the requirement for high quality and effective staff development.

What we know

Members of the school workforce have different terms and conditions regarding their employment. The School Support Staff Negotiating Body (SSSNB) deals with matters relating to their renumeration and conditions of work. The longer established School Teachers Review Body (STRB) advises the government on teachers' pay and conditions. The *Teachers' Pay and Conditions* document (2008) stipulates that

> Para 77.3 A teacher employed full-time must be available for work for 195 days in any school year, of which-
>
> (a) 190 days must be days on which he (sic) may be required to teach pupils and perform other duties; and
>
> (b) 5 days must be days on which he may only be required to perform other duties; and those 195 days must be specified by his employer or, if his employer so directs, by the head teacher. (DCSF, 2008, p131)

Teachers also have a duty to contribute to the 'professional development of other teachers and support staff'.

We know that many staff work way beyond their contracted hours. Since 1994 the STRB have undertaken surveys of a sample of school teachers and leaders to gauge their workloads. These show that the average number of hours worked in term time is high. Despite measures to reduce workload it has remained high (see Tables 4.1 and 4.2).

Table 4.1   Comparing the hours worked by teachers in a week in March (based on BMRB (*2008*), Teachers Workloads Diary Survey 2008, OME)

	1994	**1996**	**2000**	**2003**	**2008**
Primary					
Headteachers	55.4	55.7	58.9	55.5	55.2
Deputy/assistant heads	52.4	54.5	56.2	56.4	52.8
Classroom teachers	48.8	50.8	52.8	51.8	52.2
Secondary					
Headteachers	61.1	61.7	60.8	60.9	59.5
Deputy/assistant heads	56.9	56.5	58.6	56.5	58.0
Heads of faculty/department	50.7	53.0	52.9	52.7	52.9
Classroom teachers	48.9	50.3	51.3	50.8	49.9
Special					
Classroom teachers	47.5	50.0	51.2	47.6	48.3

Table 4.2   Hours worked and spent teaching (based on BMRB (*2008*), Teachers Workloads Diary Survey 2008, OME)

March 2008	**Total hours**	**Hours teaching**
Primary		
Headteachers	55.2	3.3
Deputy/assistant heads	52.8	12.4
Classroom teachers	52.2	17.2
Secondary		
Headteachers	59.5	1.9
Deputy/assistant heads	58.0	8.9
Heads of faculty/department	52.9	17.2
Classroom teachers	49.9	19.0
Special		
Classroom teachers	48.3	15.6

These measures have required the school workforce to be remodelled so that there has, for example, been a huge increase in the number of support staff. These are the actions that have happened over the last few years as part of the remodelling agenda:

1. Progressive reductions in teachers' overall hours.

2. Changes to contracts, to ensure that teachers, including headteachers:

   - do not routinely undertake administrative and clerical tasks

   - have a reasonable work–life balance

   - have a reduced burden of providing cover for absent colleagues

   - have guaranteed planning, preparation and assessment time within the school day to support their teaching, individually and collaboratively·

   - have a reasonable allocation of time in support of their leadership and management responsibilities

   - do not invigilate external examinations.

3. Changes to headteachers' contracts to ensure that they have dedicated time that recognises their significant responsibilities.

4. A concerted attack on unnecessary paperwork and bureaucratic processes for teachers and headteachers. An implementation review unit was established, featuring a panel of experienced, serving headteachers.

5. Reform of support staff roles to help teachers and support pupils. Personal administrative assistants for teachers, cover supervisors and higher level teaching assistants introduced.

6. The recruitment of new managers, including business and personnel managers, and others with experience from outside education where they have the expertise to contribute effectively to schools' leadership teams.

7. Additional resources and national change management programmes to help school leaders achieve the necessary reforms of the teaching profession and restructuring of the school workforce.

8. Monitoring of progress on delivery by the signatories of the agreement (Ofsted, 2008, annex 2).

For the sample week in March 2008, the STRB survey found about 5 per cent of teachers' working time was taken up with 'professional and associated activity'. Teachers were also found to spend about 18 hours per week teaching (about one-third of their working time and slightly higher for secondary teachers) with planning, preparation and assessment (PPA) taking up just over 30 per cent of their working time (see Table 4.3).

A report from the Institute of Public Policy Research (Margo et al., 2008) states that teachers spend only 3 per cent of their time on staff development and that they have less development time than those in other OECD countries. They suggest this is due to the limited contractual time for teachers to undertake development activities and

Table 4.3   How classroom teachers spend their time in one week (based on BMRB (*2008*), Teacher Workloads Diary Survey 2008, OME. p16)

	Primary hours	Secondary hours	Primary %	Secondary %
Teaching	17.2	19.0	33.0%	38.0%
Planning, preparation & assessment	17.0	15.2	32.5%	30.4%
Non-teaching pupil/parent contact	6.0	7.2	11.5%	14.3%
School/staff management	3.5	2.8	6.7%	5.5%
General administrative support	4.7	3.1	8.9%	6.1%
Individual/professional activity	3.2	2.3	6.1%	4.7%
Other activities	0.7	0.5	1.3%	1.0%
TOTAL	52.2	49.9	100.0%	100.0%

'because funding is devolved to schools, not teachers, and is not ring fenced, meaning that it may be used for purposes other than CPD' (p9).

The statutory 10 per cent of the working week for planning, preparation and assessment which as part of the workload agreement became statutory in September 2005, although beneficial, seems to have had a detrimental effect on time for staff development. Some headteachers are more reluctant to let people out of the classroom because of the increased disruption to pupil learning and effect on behaviour. Some secondary schools in particular either restricted or placed an embargo on staff development that required time out of lessons or away from the school. Restrictions include capping the number of staff being out of school on any one day. Local authority advisers have noticed a drop in bookings for courses because of this, seeing schools as more likely to ask for sessions to be run in their own buildings as twilights or development/INSET days instead of sending people out on courses.

Ideas for finding time

Schools must be creative in finding time for staff development during the course of the normal school day or working week. Involvement in teams, working parties, planning groups and committees – events and activities not always associated with staff development – can provide solid learning opportunities. How many of the following ideas and suggestions for finding time for staff development are already found in your workplace or would work for you in your context?

Reducing admin meetings: People spend a considerable amount of time in meetings so how can they be organised to aid development? Are they really meetings or simply briefings for the transfer of information? If the latter, there are more efficient ways to communicate. One school cut its meetings to a minimum by making more use of the online diary which all staff have access to and which is shown on a large plasma screen in the foyer and staffroom.

Meetings for staff development: A 'true' meeting implies interaction, discussion, the sharing of ideas and crucially the possibility of more than one outcome or way of achieving it. Of course, even the best planned meetings contain both interactive items and transactional ones – the important point is that the two must be differentiated, with the interactive items dominating. Having an agenda and pre-meeting tasks can mean that more is achieved in a shorter amount of time, as can be seen in this example for a departmental meeting to explore personalised learning.

The following is a list of statements designed to prompt discussion at the next departmental meeting. It is important to look at them and come along with some ideas as each person in the department will be asked to open discussion on at least one of the statements.

- There is no difference between differentiation and personalised learning.
- There is a shared definition in the department of personalised learning, which is…
- An example of a lesson I taught where I personalised the learning was…
- Personalising learning is a nice idea in theory but involves too much work in practice.
- Developing thinking skills is the key to personalising learning.
- Ultimately what matters is the exam performance of individual students.
- Developing personalised learning in the department requires us to… (Edgar, 2009, p44)

Fortnightly mornings: A secondary school has a series of staff development sessions between 8.30 and 10.00am every fortnight. All staff are able to attend as students arrive at 10.00am, instead of 9.00am. In the hour that teaching is lost, learning isn't because students have to complete e-learning tasks prepared by each department. Students without a computer at home, complete the tasks in the school's computer suite either from 9.00–10.00am or after school. Staff feedback was very positive. They felt supported in their development; they found it beneficial because it was not a one off session but continuous; they thought that mornings were a better time for learning than twilights.

Weekly mornings: A special school runs staff development for 45 minutes on Thursday mornings before pupils arrive. This training is mandatory for all staff and it includes outside presenters. The tight time limit meant that much is covered and time is used well in that people are receptive to learning because they were fresh.

Thinking dinners: One secondary school's senior leadership team of 11 people has moved from meeting on Wednesdays after school to having 'thinking dinners' and occasional '24 hour' residentials from Friday evening to Saturday lunch time. They leave school promptly, go home to change, and convene at a venue with meeting room and meal. They ensure that there are 'substantial issues on the agenda rather than trivia' and feel they achieve more because they were refreshed.

Reading groups: Some schools devote part of their regular timetabled meetings to a discussion of recent research findings or policy documents. These 'seminars' are facilitated by individuals who will circulate the necessary readings a week or so in advance. In one case the Senior Leadership Team (SLT) was considering a new book on leadership and comparing its own practice with that expounded by the theorists.

Staff planning rooms: In Norway, teachers have a space allocation in a staff planning room. Typically three or four teachers share a room in which they each have their own desk, shelves and computer. This encourages and facilitates joint planning and professional development that comes from working with and talking to others.

Using existing time well

Finding time for staff development is a challenge but are we using existing time well and doing the right things to ensure staff development happens and children's education is not affected by staff absence? For example, the Staff Development Outcomes study (SDOS) found that in schools where arrangements for covering staff undertaking training was highly organised, pupils' learning and well-being was not affected. In one school there was a central table by the staffroom and offices with neat piles of work (e.g. worksheets for everyone in the class) with clear instructions. Another school had a Teaching Environment of the Future to which classes could be relocated to use IT facilities and the learning platform, supervised by TAs.

Recruiting the right people is a good starting point. In one school, the senior leaders have discovered what it is about the staff that works and what makes a good staff member for different parts of the school. This is a result of being very self-analytical and placing a lot of emphasis on improving staff. Therefore, when recruiting, they look for people with energy and drive, the right personality, and general attributes and skills rather than specialised skill sets. They look for people who have good social skills, intelligence and who want to be leaders in preference to simply someone who can do the job. They train staff for the role once recruited.

Initial teacher education

Schools involved with initial teacher education have found that having trainees on placements is valuable. It frees up time for more staff development and is in itself a powerful development activity for the staff who support, monitor and assess them. Indeed, it can bring about a strong coaching-mentoring culture for all staff. One school has a policy of making innovations from the bottom up by starting with new staff. Another school liaises with good quality universities which are highly selective so that they are sent strong trainees. This benefits the departments in which they work during training and when there are teacher vacancies the school has the pick of the crop without the costs of advertising and interviewing.

Developing through training

Some schools run courses which others buy in to. This is seen as a great development opportunity for the staff that plan and run the training, as well as providing a service and extra income.

Staff development notice board and newsletter

Staff development can be made very visible through having a board in the staffroom with notices about courses and resources such as documents on behaviour management, a Teachers TV schedule, local authority training programmes, the staff development policy and the TDA teacher standards poster. The Staff Development Leader may also produce leaflets advertising and reminding staff of twilight sessions.

In one of the SDOS case study schools there was a CPD Update newsletter, produced by the CPD leader as part of his strategy to maintain its high profile in the school. The newsletter has articles on hot topics e.g. 'Assessment for Learning: what's it all about?'; notices for forthcoming sessions; lists staff going on external courses; gives brief feedback from courses, welcomes new trainees; thanks staff who are leaving; lists Teachers TV programmes and reminds people about keeping a professional portfolio. The first edition of the newsletter featured an article about how staff development is defined in the school, why it is important for the school and the individual. It also outlines and emphasises what development activities are available within the school.

Remodelling

Schools are remodelling their workforce, distributing leadership and responsibilities across more people. This should free up time for staff development. Schools have cover supervisors or higher level teaching assistants who cover classes. In one school, sixth formers are trained as 'cover students' to work with support staff in order to help with subject knowledge. The cover students enjoy the role and the cover supervisors appreciate their subject knowledge to support the delivery of the lesson. The pupils respect and admire the cover students and said that they have a better learning experience compared with other cover arrangements.

Shadowing

Schools' approaches to investing in staff should be long term and this involves planning ahead. One school prides itself on recognising the contributions of staff at all stages of their career and through an ongoing shadowing system adapting to people wanting time off or to scale down because of dependents. A classroom assistant (CA) who is due to retire is being shadowed by another CA to ensure her experience is tapped. The school now has assistant heads to create another tier of capable leaders for when deputies move on.

PPA

Time for planning, preparation and assessment (PPA) is a great opportunity for staff development although it has meant less off-site staff development during the working week. In one school, the CAs cover PPA by taking all the classes for the first 30 minutes each morning, thus enabling teachers to plan, assess and find resources together. Other schools block the PPA of staff in the same teams so that they can work together.

Overstaffing

Some schools have a policy of overstaffing so that all absence for staff development or sickness is covered internally so that any disruption to children's education is minimised. In one school there are 24 full-time teachers for just 16 classes so the extra teachers can take over classes for development time or staff sickness as well as teaching groups.

In another primary school an additional teacher with a high level of experience and skill is based in each two class year group. She plans with the two class-assigned teachers, covering their PPA and development time, and supporting their practice by modelling and team teaching.

Blue skies thinking

At a time when many schools complain that there is 'no time for staff development' we need to ask hard questions about how contractual time is being spent, especially the five additional 'development' days. The STRB reports have shown consistently that teachers work on average about 52 hours per week (senior staff longer) during term time (see Table 4.1). Although actual teaching only accounts for about a third of this time (see Table 4.2), teaching is very demanding and high intensity – a performance – and this is reflected in the levels of absence and staff stress. The intensity levels and the performance nature of teaching creates additional demands and the Health and Safety Executive have reported that 41 per cent of teachers rate their job as high stress, compared to 32 per cent of nurses. Stress is the single largest cause of occupational ill health in England. In 2008 over half of the teaching workforce (58 per cent) took sickness absence. A total of 2,754,700 teaching days were lost, with those people on sickness absence being away for an average of 8.7 days, which is 4.6 per cent of the teaching year. Workload and stress are constantly noted as reasons for leaving teaching, with schools in challenging circumstances worst affected. It is perhaps unsurprising that there is little time or inclination to engage in staff development activity, contractual or otherwise. The workload and stress issues are interrelated and need to be addressed not only for the health of the school workforce but in order to better accommodate the requirement for high quality and effective staff development.

There has been much talk over recent years about 'workforce remodelling' but this does not appear to include teachers and their patterns of employment. Many have argued that the school year should no longer be largely based on nineteenth century notions, centred as they were on the need to collect the summer harvest. It is time to remodel the teachers' year! Radical change is needed which we feel would benefit all learners – both teachers and pupils – but which would also benefit staff welfare and well-being, and, most importantly, enhance their ability to engage in meaningful staff development. If the length of the pupil year remains at 190 days, we would wish to restrict teachers to a 40 hour week and therefore expect some of the 28 days (on top of the 30 days holiday that many people outside schools get a year) to be used for staff development purposes.

We need to ask if meetings and development/INSET days are being spent sufficiently on staff development and what is the best way of utilising that time? If, as our research suggests, extra days of holiday result from a greater use of twilights rather than whole INSET days, can't we therefore reasonably expect teachers to undertake some development opportunities in their 'own' time? Of course many staff do use their own time at weekends, half-terms and summer holidays for development – and schools are permitted to pay individuals for such time (e.g. for attending approved courses) – but should there not be a greater expectation for all staff to do so?

Of course some development activities will need to take place when students are in session. For example, teachers stress the value of classroom observation and feedback which some argue has the greatest impact on professional growth and change (Bubb, 2005). Cordingley and Temperley (2006) draw on an extensive synthesis of research into what makes staff development effective and note that 'collaborative CPD is *more likely* than individual CPD to result in learning gains for pupils as well as for teachers'. Collaboration need not only take place when pupils are present. Action-research, learning communities, networks and other collaborative, school-based staff development may be more effective than traditional off-site courses but do they always have to take place during school time?

Also we know that the most effective types of development are those that directly meet individual needs as well as school-based needs so a more personalised approach to staff development is needed that is closely linked to Performance Management. This can be linked to the five training days. Visits to other schools can be a powerful form of learning too (Atherton, 2005) and many of these activities can take place outside of official school time (190 days) and therefore have no disruptive effect on pupil learning. We need to think creatively about making and using time for staff development especially at a time when the heavy workload of teachers means that it is increasingly being squeezed out.

Many companies expect staff to undertake up to ten working days per annum on staff development and for many professional bodies, continuing membership is dependent on undertaking so many hours of professional development. However, it is salutary to compare teachers' holiday time with other comparable professions and ask if some of this 'holiday' time might be devoted to staff development. Shorter holidays, especially over the summer, could have considerable benefits for teachers' and other staff's learning and development but also for pupils as many studies have documented the amount of 'learning loss' which takes place over the long summer break.

What might new models of the school staff year look like? Have a look at Table 4.4. We think they are worth serious consideration given the present intensity of term time, the growing evidence of disruption to pupil learning, teacher absence and stress levels and the squeezing out of term time staff development. To create more time for staff development we can alter the existing teacher year by, for example, utilising some PPA time for staff development, training and deploying more cover supervisors, employing more teachers (supernumeraries) and making greater use of the regulation which allows payment for staff development outside of the 195 days (e.g. during holidays). Or we could simply increase the number of development days. Our view, however, is that such approaches, given existing resources and budgets, will only be partially successful: we need blue skies thinking to introduce new, more radical twenty-first century approaches to conditions of service. This will be of great benefit to both school staff and the pupils they serve.

One suggestion has been simply to replace the current five INSET or development days with 20 days of compulsory CPD (Margo et al., 2008). This Institute for Public Policy Research report suggests that 'Ten days of this training would take place in the school (with the expectation that schools will facilitate this) and ten days outside via external providers, conferences, school visits or even visits to other countries' (Ibid., p11). The report however is less clear on where these extra 15 days

Table 4.4   A new model of the teachers' year

Present	Option 1	Option 2
190 teaching days (10 hr days)	190 teaching days (7–8 hr days)	190 teaching days (7–8 hr days)
0–5 INSET days	5 INSET days	0 INSET days
8 bank holidays	8 bank holidays	8 bank holidays
104 – weekend	104 – weekend	104 – weekend
58–63 – holidays, some spent ill	30 – holidays	30 – holidays
	28 days for development	33 days for development

would come from. Our alternative model is more specific about where the time for staff development would be found.

In addition to a reduction in the number of days for holidays, we suggest a decrease in the number of hours that teachers work each week during term time. Workload is a widespread concern in schools and it is not uncommon for staff to suffer from stress, exhaustion and burn out. Limiting staff to a 7–8 hour day in term time will be a challenge and involve a cultural change which headteachers, senior leaders and governing bodies would need to monitor carefully. This change of working pattern would take some time to implement but would become established as the norm as new teachers entered the remodelled profession. Staff development and training would not normally be expected to take place during the school day: it would be the exception not the norm. Currently where training takes place during the busy school week, especially after a day's teaching, it is likely to exacerbate not improve the situation.

Our new model of the teachers' year has the option of removing the five development days altogether from the contracted year and using those days for further development during school 'holidays'. Most professional groups are entitled to 30 days annual leave and introducing the same arrangement for teachers would create additional time for development. We believe that the intensity of the school year often means that teachers spend some of their long 'holidays' recovering and recuperating. Our model of the teacher's year would mean this is less likely to occur and that up to 28 days (option 1) or 33 days (option 2) could then be used for development.

However, development days in one form or another are likely to be around for some time yet so how can they be used to best effect? It is to this that we next turn.

5

How to make the most of development days

> **This chapter covers:**
>
> - **What we know**
> - **Making the most of development days**
> - **Planning the days**

Unlike many other professions, including most recently those in the Learning and Skills/Further Education sector, where individuals are expected to accrue or 'clock up' 30 hours of professional development annually, school teachers are allocated five additional days when pupils are not on site. They are known as training, INSET, professional, Baker or development days. The latter is the term we prefer because they should be about staff development. These five days form a significant part of the contracted time available for teachers' professional development so schools need to ensure this time is being used well. Recent research evidence suggests that in many cases it is not.

What we know

The Staff Development Outcomes study (Bubb et al., 2009) found that just four out of ten senior staff and teachers said that their school used their development days as five whole days and this resulted in extra days of holiday for most staff as the missing days were usually converted into after-school sessions. It's a bigger issue in secondaries with only a fifth of secondary school respondents saying that all five days were used. Some people said that, 'INSET days with all staff together are like gold dust' and the value of having a prolonged time to learn and develop together as a whole staff was seen as invaluable. Other people converted different numbers of whole training days into twilight sessions or private study as these examples illustrate:

- *This year we have disaggregated one development day into two hours of twilight for staff celebration and four hours of personal professional learning time.*

- *We have one whole school development day, 12 sessions from 2.30 to 4.00pm on Wednesdays when pupils leave early and a development day with staff from other local schools.*

- *Two whole days are disaggregated and used for private study time (including twilights) to suit needs.*

- *We have completely personalised our five days. Colleagues are asked to self direct 20 hours of CPD (this can be pretty much anything as long as it reflects the School Improvement Plan (SIP)). The school directs the remaining ten hours – these are usually extended workshops run from 2.30 to 6.00 on Wednesdays when students go home early. Colleagues are asked to keep a log of their activities which the CPD co-ordinator monitors and quality assures. Staff are also actively encouraged to deliver sessions and these count as 'double' in terms of their 20 hours.*

How a development day is spent

We found that not all of an INSET day is spent on training and development. Only a third of senior staff and nearly four out of ten teachers reported that the whole of their last training day was used for this (see Table 5.1). One in eight teachers in secondary schools reported spending *none* of the last closure day on training and development.

When asked how useful development days had been over the last 12 months, over a third of senior staff thought they were 'very useful' in helping people develop (see Table 5.2). This was in contrast to teachers and support staff who found them less useful: about a quarter said they were 'of little use'.

The most useful days were seen as the ones which gave ideas that could be used directly in the classroom, provided opportunities to meet with others and discuss issues or helped to build teamwork and ensure 'everyone was singing from the same hymn sheet'. Special school staff felt that too much of their 'development' time was spent on necessary but routine refresher health and safety training.

Those people who were critical of development days suggested there was a need for them to focus more on training/development and less on administration. Some said the days were used mainly for promoting new initiatives, which were not always tailored to the school's needs or to their own professional development priorities.

Table 5.1 Proportion of the last INSET day spent on training and development (Bubb et al., 2009, p. 41)

	Whole day	¾ day	½ day	¼ day	None	Total (%)
Senior	33	17	30	9	7	100
Teachers	39	25	23	6	4	100

(Senior = 397; Teachers = 466)

Table 5.2 Views of usefulness of development days in the last 12 months (Bubb et al., 2009, p. 42)

	Very useful	Useful	Of little use	A waste of time	Total (%)
Senior staff	36	57	5	0	100
Teachers	16	57	24	3	100
Support staff	13	45	24	8	100

(Senior = 397; Teachers = 466; Support = 749)

Making the most of development days

Organising the five development days a year is a huge task. How can you please everyone? Clearly, there is a lot to think about when organising the days to ensure that the time is used to best effect. You need to decide whether to run training after school rather than on development days. Some advantages and disadvantages of each are listed in Table 5.3.

Table 5.3   Pros and cons to having after school sessions instead of whole development days

Advantages	Disadvantages
Frees up days for extra holiday	Staff are tired
More frequent – little and often	Some staff won't be able to attend
Easier to organise	Lose time with latecomers
Easier to meet individual needs	Too short to gain much benefit
Gets people together more often	Hard to lead, because staff are tired
Smaller groups	Hard to get external speakers
	Nothing special
	Few spare after school slots available

It helps if you return to first principles: thinking about the kinds of development activities which make the most difference to practice. We believe that these are:

- based on dialogue about teaching and learning

- collaborative – learning from, with and for others

- rooted in everyday work and current priorities

- focused on solving problems

- personalised to individual learning preferences and needs

- sustained over time and accumulative rather than based on one-offs.

Awareness-raising events are useful for absorbing information and updating knowledge but are not per se likely to lead to improvements in how people work or become better at what they do.

When to hold them

Most schools hold them on the first or last days of a term or half-term. This allows an easing into or from a holiday and allows pupils longer breaks but this timing is not always conducive to learning as staff are either tired if it's the end of a term, or want to spend time on preparation if it's the start. It also means that outside trainers are hard to book and expensive.

You don't have to hold them on Mondays or Fridays. A day in the middle of a week and term has the tonic effect of a change. A networked learning community of six schools held a joint training day on a Wednesday in the third week of September. This was a date when they could get a large high quality venue and inspirational speakers at low prices. Parents liked this as they could treat their children to a day out when there weren't crowds or organise child care. Another school found it effective to put two training days together for intensive learning. A TA said, 'It was great being able to immerse oneself in it'. Over the year, it's best to choose different days of the week so that timetables don't suffer. For instance, if all your training days are on Mondays this means that classes timetabled for that day of the week miss six out of 40 sessions – an eighth – including the May Day bank holiday.

The length of the development day is also worth considering: it does not need to match the pupils' school day timings but could start and finish later depending on what you want to achieve and who you would like to involve. If midday supervisors are used to working over the lunch period, ask whether they could come at a different time or organise development activities for them during the hours they normally work. Parts of the day could be for self-study or research which could be done off-site or in different parts of the building. A structure for this such as meeting afterwards to pool learning will ensure that people stay focused.

How to spend them

It's handy to get ideas of how other schools have spent development days. Most choose to focus on a school improvement plan priority, have an inspiring input for the whole staff and then split into groups for more interaction and collaboration to meet individual needs. It's beneficial for people to talk about the work or projects they've been doing within their roles: that's good development for them and for the audience.

Conferences

Some schools have gone as a staff to an event: a conference or an education show such as BETT. This has the benefits of having a shared experience but also capturing learning from things that others have seen. For instance, the TES Education Show not only has hundreds of stalls with people to speak to and things to look at and try out but seminars on a host of different topics by top speakers.

Day trip

Taking the whole staff to a museum, gallery, town or activity centre can be a good way to kick-start a school project or trip. This needs structuring with groups being carefully selected, well briefed and expected to bring back different things. A plenary where the learning and experiences are pooled can increase the intellectual and social capital and give a purpose to everyone's endeavours, not least a very detailed risk assessment drawing on many people's insights.

Governors' school

Governors in one local authority have a Saturday training event in a school where they take the role of pupils. The day is set up like a school day with assembly, lessons and break time and teachers and advisers teach lessons. Towards the end of each lesson, people come out of role to ask questions. People find this great fun and very informative as it gives a good insight into so many aspects of school life.

Sharing with other schools

In one local authority all the local secondary schools shared a development day, organising 60 workshops across nine school sites. This met subject specific needs in that for instance all the PE teachers and coaches went to the same site. There were generic sessions on topics such as time management and behaviour for learning. The library and resource centre staff met with each other and had a session from the school library association. Admin staff were able to have training on new systems. Site staff had a series of sessions related to health and safety. As well as being able to choose activities that were more personalised, it proved to be very good development for workshop leaders. A tight supportive structure was given to help them, such as:

1. input

2. activities

3. discussion

4. action planning.

People found it useful to get into another school, meet staff from other settings and have their specific needs met. The networking was powerful and continued beyond the event.

Visiting another school

Some schools send their staff en masse to another organisation to see how it works. The impetus for one was the planning of a new building so the whole staff went to visit a school on a recently opened new site to see exactly what the issues were. This enabled everyone to contribute in detail to the aspect of the building design and resources that related to their role. It helped them prepare for the significant changes and disruptions ahead. They also gained a great deal from seeing another school in action on an ordinary day.

Visiting other schools

For one school's development day 80 members of staff visited 60 other schools (Atherton, 2005). To make staff development a more personalised experience for all, they matched visits with performance management objectives and identified development needs of each member of staff, not just teachers. The organiser felt that people had most to learn from schools in a similar position and used the City Challenge *Families of Schools* document (DfES, 2006) to find ones with comparable types of pupils. Local and national figures were consulted on where to go. Many schools provided detailed negotiated programmes that included opportunities for discussion with staff and students, and observations of lessons.

There was a well thought through structure, which was explained at a whole staff meeting. A part-time member of the admin team was employed for extra hours to liaise between staff and schools. Everyone outlined what they hoped to gain from their visit and how this linked with the school development plan priorities. Each person agreed to try to find some things to share with colleagues: 640 new ideas were found! Many ideas on teaching and learning were picked up from primary schools. People in the admin team found it interesting to see how different systems worked. All staff were inspired and then took responsibility for elements of school improvement by drawing up action plans and posting them on the school intranet. The results of their improvements were discussed at the next development day seven weeks later. Interestingly, some of the ideas gleaned from other schools weren't new at all, but things that were being done by people within the school. Do you know what pearls of practice lie down the corridor?

Planning the days

Development days require a great deal of planning. Firstly you need to decide on the focus. Why is it a priority? What do you want people to get out of the session? As with any lesson, a focus on the learning objectives is key – but not very easy. You might want to refine it by asking yourself what you hope the new person, the experienced and the seen-it-all-before cynic will get out of it.

Who

Who is the training for? You'll want to be as inclusive as possible but whoever comes needs to feel that there's a point to them being there. One school held two consecutive development days for the whole staff at a hotel with residential facilities. Nobody found the training useful although most had a nice time. A senior teaching assistant found it a waste of time because 'a lot of it went over me and my girls' heads' and 'it made me feel stressed and violently sick' because she couldn't understand what was being talked about. In an attempt to include the whole school workforce, too little attention had been paid to addressing the needs and taking account of the feelings of a range of staff.

Who is going to lead and contribute to the session? External expertise can be motivating and take the pressure off school leaders but it can be expensive and not tailored to your staffs' needs. One school bought two days' of staff training from an outside provider when there were highly experienced people working in the school who probably could have done this just as well. It was very expensive, in money and time. Had the school used its own expertise, needs may have been met in a more bespoke fashion at a greatly reduced cost.

Whomever is involved needs to be briefed so that they can plan their input to have the desired impact. Briefing could include:

- date

- audience

- topic – the desired impact, with information about what has already been covered and where people are at now (the range) in the focus area

- style

- timings – as exact as possible

- venue, room arrangement, technology, materials

- dress code

- travel

- things to be aware of.

See Table 5.4 for an example.

Table 5.4   Briefing for trainer

Topics	Briefing
Date	Thursday 28 January
Audience	110–60 teachers and about 50 support staff
Topic	Managing your workload
The desired impact	For people to have the big picture of national workload issues, how other schools are addressing them and to consider their workload and what to improve
What has already been covered	Nothing since workforce remodelling 3 years ago
Where people are at now	Some teachers have a PM objective about managing workload better. Most staff feel overworked
Subsidiary impact	To inspire people to think positively and do something About the issue (stop moaning!)
Style	Lively presentation with some interaction within tables. Sensitivity to the mix of staff – all to be valued
Timings	9.40–10.45, after an intro at 9.30 followed by a break and then workshop groups. Please arrive by 9.00 and stay around until about 11.15 to answer questions
Dress code	Smart casual
Venue	School hall
Room arrangement	Tables of 6–8, mixed support staff and teachers; fruit and water on tables
Technology	PC and interactive whiteboard with internet connection and speakers, lapel microphone
Materials	Flip chart, handouts, Post-its, poster paper
Things to be aware of	Possible hostility from a few active union reps
Travel	8 mins walk from station, car parking available

Style

Think about what sort of training you have enjoyed and got something from – the two do not necessarily go together. What were the elements? What has worked for your staff in the past? Take account of the audience's preferred learning styles and make any presentations appeal in visual, auditory and kinaesthetic ways. Some people hate being expected to do an activity every five minutes. Nor do many people like hundreds of PowerPoint slides being flashed up, or speakers who recite every word of every slide. Most people like a bit of pace, a chance to talk through issues, and a facilitator with personality and a lot of humour who can keep control of the group, especially that pain who keeps asking such stupid questions.

How long have you got? Are your aims realistic for the time allocated? How are you going to achieve your intended outcomes? How are you going to make sure that people feel their time is spent well? Will they come prepared? Do you need an agenda? What snags can you foresee?

You need to think what is manageable within the time available, and then try to set some realistic success criteria. These will be different for different groups of people so it's quite a good idea to imagine what these might be. There are bound to be a range, including ongoing general ones such as people having time to think more deeply about things, enjoy themselves or having the chance to talk to each other. It's important to think about confidence as well; learning something new can be uncomfortable and worrying. Maintain confidence levels by reminding people about their strengths, progress they're making and how far they've come.

Where

The venue in which you run any staff development is a surprisingly significant factor in its success. Going off-site lends an air of specialness and stops people nipping off at break times to get a few jobs done but it will normally have hassle factors such as booking, cost and travel. Hotels often sound appealing but can disappoint, with training rooms that are stuck in the basement with no natural light and technology that is dodgy or expensive – or both. Some schools hold development days in attractive locations, including ones abroad having found good deals out of season; one infamously having to cancel an £18,000 two day event for 80 staff in Marbella after a media furore.

If you stay in school, unless you have a training area you have to choose between using a classroom, the staffroom or the hall, none of which is ideal. The perfect scenario is to have a room with the technology you need and good acoustics that is spacious enough to have people sitting in groups around tables, but not so big that personal contact between the presenter and each person is made impossible.

Refreshments

As Napoleon said, an army marches on its stomach. Food matters: it can really help training go well. Placing fruit or sweets and water on tables costs little in comparison to the feel-good factor engendered. One person puts lollipops on chairs not only as a treat but to get people quiet as they suck. Something nice to eat before a session is often a good way to ensure punctuality, especially if people know that the goodies will run out before the session starts.

Providing lunch is not just a treat during a development day; it provides a forum for continuing conversations and networking. This may just be sandwiches or you might want to order a takeaway. There may be a theme: Chinese for Chinese New Year. Again any cost needs to be balanced with looking at the alternative: if you provide nothing people won't mingle and will wander off physically as well as mentally. A treat – the draw of a raffle, wine, cake, a memory stick – at the end may be nice too and might discourage people sloping off early.

Grouping

If you're having the whole staff together, think about groupings carefully. Three or four people per table means that all are engaged, whereas if numbers go bigger some people are bound to dominate and others take a back seat. When numbers go over six what tends to happen is that the group breaks into two simply because it's quite hard for six people to talk and work together, especially with background noise from other tables. You might want to group people in order to get rid of the usual cliques. Integrating staff is really important, but you need to think whether it is best to sit support staff together or to mix them in with teachers. The aim and the focus of the session will help you in this. For instance, in a session looking at workload it could be beneficial for teachers to work with teachers, teaching assistants to work with teaching assistants, office staff to work with office staff. On the other hand, how interesting would it be if each table had one or two people from each group? If an experienced teacher, a newish teacher, a teaching assistant, a midday supervisor and somebody from the office work together they will have a rare opportunity to get to know each other. This could help them appreciate each other's roles and pressure points, especially in a session about workload and work–life balance.

Try to mix the groups up during the training so that people get to work and talk with a range of colleagues. Some people strongly dislike moving and may even refuse to. Don't worry; this isn't the end of the world. You want to avoid any regrouping taking too much time and being a distraction. Do things briskly and with simple instructions: people with the letter A in their first name please stand and find a seat at the next table going clockwise.

Structure

As we know from any teaching a good lesson has variety in it so you'll want to intersperse participant listening with talking and doing. The structure in Figure 5.1 might be useful. Listening to the same voice can become a little tedious, so it might be useful to present in pairs leading on different sections so that the participants hear different voices. It also takes the pressure off individuals, giving presenters time to draw breath and re-energise for their next bit. This is really important, because it is the leaders of the session who will set the pace and keep motivation levels high. If they are feeling tired, stressed or uncertain it will have a detrimental effect on the group's learning.

How should you start the session? Think of what will work best at the time of day you will be doing the training. It's really important to make a strong impact to set the

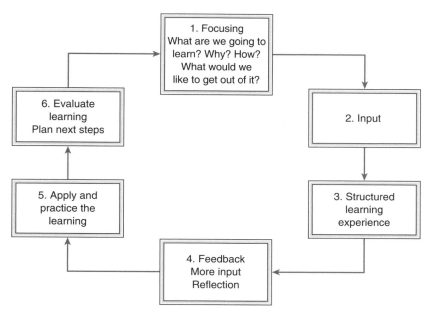

Figure 5.1   Structure for training

session off to a good start – and that includes starting on time even if not everyone is there. This sets the tone. Obviously you don't want to get completely stuck-in with only half the participants there, so do a short warm-up activity that makes people feel that their time is being spent well – and sends a message to latecomers that punctuality does matter.

Give the group a clear purpose and outcome for the session, and the big picture – what is going to happen. It can then be quite useful to give people a chance to discuss and note down any specific things that they as individuals want to get out of the session. This gets their head in gear, helps them focus on the topic in hand. Writing individual wants on Post-it notes means that people can stretch their legs in bringing them to a compilation board. A couple of people might be asked to sort the Post-it notes so that the lead presenter can see at a glance the main things upon which to focus. For instance, in a session on lesson observation skills this activity showed that people felt quite comfortable with the actual process of observation, but needed more help in giving feedback afterwards. So the presenters adapted the pitch at which they were aiming and personalised the learning by tweaking what they were going to do: allowing more time to some bits and fast tracking over others. It's handy to tick the Post-it notes when the issue has been covered, showing explicitly that these individual needs have been met.

Handouts

What about handouts? If you have some, what will be on them and when will you give them out? As a participant, we want them presented together, but as trainers we don't want people to read ahead. Aren't these just the sorts of dilemmas you face when teaching classes? Yes, but unfortunately you cannot tell adults off when they don't do as they're asked. Think about how you will deal with mobile phones going off, latecomers and people who wander off the point.

Activities

Learning – be it for children or adults – needs to be active, and thus it is important that any training session has within it activities for participants to do. These could include:

- diamond 9 to discuss priorities

- post-its for brainstorming and sorting

- discussing in pairs, trios, etc.

- gallery – wander round the room looking at items and then discuss them

- role play

- concrete experience of what is being learned, e.g. working out a maths problem.

Make sure you explain any activities clearly – and why you are asking people to do them. Nobody likes doing activities just for the sake of them, so try to communicate the purpose behind them. It's useful to have a range of tasks for individuals, pairs, trios and larger groups and for them to last different lengths of time. If you give people too long they will nip out to the loo, check their phone or generally go off task. A good rule of thumb is to tell people that they have a fraction less time to do the task than is entirely realistic because that will motivate them to get cracking. Note the end of the activity time on the board so that people stay on track. This is useful for the presenter too, because often during group activities somebody will want to raise an issue with you individually, and then time can slip away.

Be selective in the amount of feedback you ask for. Reporting back can be very time-consuming, repetitive and boring so think of a range of ways to do this such as:

- collating points as you go around eavesdropping or working with groups

- one or two points per group

- one group feeding back to another group

- making a poster, then passing to other groups or displaying.

Video clips are very useful. Teachers TV has made presentations on many issues for staff development leaders to use. For instance, there's a primary and secondary one for structuring a 45-minute CPD session on behaviour. It contains six clips from programmes shot in schools, and each is only three or four minutes long. To accompany the clips there are short programme summaries and discussion starters written on PowerPoint. The clips don't need to be watched in any particular order, and the presentation and discussion points can be adapted to suit the priorities of individual schools. There are web links to view the full programmes and additional resources. All in all, this is a super resource.

 Activity: Watch *Secondary Work/Life Balance: CPD Leaders* **(www.teachers.tv/cpdleaders), which has clips of:**

- A new head of department balances work and a young family
- A TA wants to stop working through his breaks
- A part-time RE teacher is effectively working full-time
- A business manager must learn to delegate
- An ICT teacher has created a time-saving 'homework by email' system
- A headteacher tries to reduce his stress levels.

Which of the clips and discussion starters would you use, which would you adapt and how, and which would you cut and why?

The plenary

Keeping to time is tricky. Finishing early is never a problem but over-running is a big no-no, so you will need strategies for moving things on. In your plan you might want to distinguish absolute must-dos from items that can be omitted if you run out of time. No matter how well you plan, you will have to think on your feet. Don't apologise for having no time for a certain activity; it will make that part appear highly attractive, and people will feel cheated. Pull the learning together in a slick way with a few minutes to spare and everyone will be happy.

Fragmented 'one-shot' INSET days at which staff listen passively to 'experts' rarely make a difference. Having a day for real development where everyone (or almost everyone) feels that they've spent their time well and are inspired to do things even better than before can make a remarkable difference. The five development days are like gold dust!

PART B

MAKING STAFF DEVELOPMENT COUNT

6

How to plan for impact

This chapter covers:

- What we know
- Understanding what staff development is
- How does impact happen?
- Levels of impact
- What sort of impact are you looking for?
- Where to find evidence of impact
- Planning to make a difference
- Value for money
- Dissemination

Evaluating the difference staff development makes is important but it's complex. Exposure to and participation in development activities may or may not bring about change to individuals' beliefs, values, attitudes and behaviours. These changes to individuals may or may not lead to changes in the classroom. And these changes may or may not lead to improvement in pupil outcomes.

What we know

Many factors influence children and young people's achievement and it is difficult to find evidence that isolates the link between staff development and achievement. People thus struggle with impact evaluation. It is the weakest link in the training and development cycle (Figure 2.1). Indeed, some schools don't even try to evaluate it, taking for granted that doing lots of training and development activities will automatically result in better teaching and learning. We found in the *Staff Development Outcomes Study* (Bubb et al., 2009) that 70 per cent of teachers and 53 per cent of support staff reported that the impact of their training and development was evaluated at their school. One headteacher said that she knew that the school's achievements in pupil standards and value added progress were very high – and that they were strongly influenced by staff development. She trusted staff to implement improvements as a result of training, and thought that forms and procedures to evaluate impact were unnecessary and could be counter-productive because staff would feel that they were being policed. She was more concerned to ensure that staff felt supported and trusted than ensuring that all training was of a high quality and had a positive impact. Some heads need to be convinced that it is a good use of resources to evaluate impact, but not necessarily by form-filling.

Table 6.1 How the impact of training and development is evaluated – teachers and support staff (%) (Bubb et al., 2009, p37)

	Teachers	Support staff
Evaluation form	41	41
Verbal/discussion	48	7
Observation	27	13
Performance management	36	3

(Teachers = 466; Support = 749)

Much evaluation is impressionistic and anecdotal – 'we just know that things are better'. Long term impact is rarely considered. The impact of staff development is rarely evaluated against the intended impact and any unplanned gains. In general, people just fill in an evaluation form after a training event but Table 6.1 shows the most common forms.

Evaluating staff development and its impact should not be burdensome and require lots of paperwork. The benefits need to outweigh the burden. One system for monitoring and evaluating impact that worked well in a primary school was an evaluation diary, which teachers wrote fortnightly and TAs wrote weekly. As well as writing about how pupils were doing, staff wrote about how they were implementing their own learning from development activities and the difference this was making to the children. This was a valuable way to see what was working, and meant that training needs could be met very quickly, and for the benefit of children. All staff interviewed were happy to write it – and seemed to enjoy both the process and the dialogue it engendered with the head and deputy.

A secondary leader felt that his school's staff development planning and evaluation forms (see Table 6.2 for our version) aided impact because people explained how they were going to use what they had learned. The evaluation form was completed within a week of a development activity and then again after two months in order to judge longer term impact. Staff were asked to write the costs of the activity, including cover, to remind them of the financial value of training. Although some people completed the forms more efficiently than others, the general view of the process was positive: a teacher said, 'It's useful to make you think about what you want to do in the future … an opportunity to think "what can I do to develop that?"'.

So what can be done? We think that evaluating impact is important. The first step is to understand what staff development is – and what it's not.

Understanding what staff development is

A key obstacle to a better appreciation of the impact of staff development lies in the way that it is conventionally defined. Many people think of staff development as activities to be engaged in rather than as the actual development of their knowledge and expertise, which may (or may not) result from their participation in such activities. They conceive of staff development in terms of inputs and not as the changes effected in their thinking and practice. There is little reference to outcomes – what will happen as a result of development activity.

Table 6.2 Development activity form – application/planning, evaluation, planning and impact

A. APPLICATION	Development activity:			
Name:	Type of activity: Observation/Visit/Course/Study time/Meeting time/Other			
Venue:	Address:		Date:	Time:
Cost:	Cover required:		Travel cost:	Total:

Baseline:

Predicted impact of this activity on you:

Pupils:

Other staff:

Which targets does it relate to?   PM: SIP: Other:

Team leader's comments

I agree to the application and confirm funding arrangements are correct.

Team leader signature: Date:

Applicant signature: Date:

B. EVALUATION – complete within 5 working days of the activity

Did the CPD activity take place as planned? Yes/No
If No, please state why

How would you rate the activity on a 1–4 scale? (1 = Excellent)	Useful	Relevance	Value for money

---

What did you gain?

Unexpected gains?

Networks made (name, contact details):

C. PLANNING What are you going to do as a result of this CPD activity? What help do you need? What are you going to disseminate?	When?	Why?

D. IMPACT – team leader evaluation to be completed after 6 weeks

What impact has it had on the individual and/or the subject/team/school?

What has been the impact on pupils?

Next steps:

Has the dissemination happened?   Yes/No   To whom?

Signed: Date:

This misconception is encouraged by the definition on the TDA website:

> Continuing professional development (CPD) consists of reflective activity designed to improve an individual's attributes, knowledge, understanding and skills. It supports individual needs and improves professional practice. (www.tda.gov.uk/cpd)

In our view staff development itself is not one activity, or set of activities. It is not definable as a course, a series of courses, a programme of training or study, or even as a set of learning experiences. Rather, staff development is the upshot or outcome that may result from any or all of these activities and from the individual's reflection on day-to-day experience of doing the job.

How does impact happen?

A common way of looking at impact is that staff learning, attitudes or beliefs change first which leads to a change in their practice, resulting in an improvement in student learning or well-being.

Staff learning, attitudes or beliefs change

which leads to

Change in their practice

resulting in

Improvement in student learning or well-being.

However, Guskey considers that it rarely happens that way in practice:

> The more typical order of change in practice is first, student learning, second, attitudes and beliefs last. And the reason that it is so, is that it is experience that shapes the attitudes and beliefs; it's not the other way around. (Guskey, 2005, p7)

Change in staff practice

... resulting in ...

Improvement in student learning or well-being

... which leads to ...

Change in staff learning, attitudes or beliefs.

This rings true and fits in with Michael Fullan's work on school improvement. People change when they see that the new skills they try out make a difference to pupils.

The key message from this is that the most important element is not the initial input or training but the putting things into practice and follow-up. For instance, we've probably all been on computer training where we've learned to use a programme such as Excel but it's only when we start using spreadsheets in our real work that we need help to put into practice what we did in training. That's when we need people to help and answer questions. Another key message from this is that any training or input needs to be quickly followed by a chance to put learning into practice ideally in people's everyday work.

Joyce and Showers (2002) also concluded that for training to be truly effective it needs to include the following five components or stages:

- theory – where the new approach is explained and justified

- demonstration – to give a model of how this can be put into practice

- practice – so that the teacher can try out the new approach

- feedback on how well the new approach is working

- coaching – to help the teacher discuss the teaching in a supportive environment and consider how it might be improved.

Their research showed that, without the opportunity to receive feedback and coaching, there is no measurable impact on classroom practice. However, once these two components are added, in particular the final coaching stage, there is a large and measurable impact on practice.

This is why activities that span a period in time are more effective that one-offs. The opportunity for collaboration with others who have been through the same training will help too.

Training part 1

2 weeks to try specific things out with the support of others

Training part 2

2 weeks to try specific things out with the support of others

Training part 3

Embed practice with the support of others

If impact evaluation is built in from the start, rather than as an after-thought, then it is more likely to make a difference. Plan target outcomes before you engage in a development activity. This requires a clear picture of what things are like before the activity takes place (the baseline) and a vision of how things should look when it is completed (the impact). Wouldn't it be great if there was a form that covered the application/planning, evaluation, planning and impact stages of development? Our attempt can be seen in Table 6.2.

Levels of impact

Thomas Guskey has done some important work in the field of impact evaluation. He considers that there are five levels of impact evaluation with improved pupil outcomes being the desired result. These five levels, shown in Table 6.3, are:

1. Participants' reactions

2. Participants' learning

3. Organisation support and change

4. Participants' use of new knowledge and skills

5. Student learning outcomes.

Table 6.3   Five levels of professional development evaluation (taken from Guskey, T. (2002) 'Does it make a difference? Evaluating professional development', *Educational Leadership*, March: 45–51)

Evaluation level	What questions are addressed?	How will information be gathered?	What is measured?	How will information be used?
Participants' reactions	Did they like it? Was their time spent well? Did the material make sense? Will it be useful? Was the leader knowledgeable and helpful? Were the refreshments fresh and tasty? Was the room the right temperature? Were the chairs comfortable?	Questionnaires administered at the end of each session	Initial satisfaction with the experience	To improve programme design and delivery
Participants' learning	Did participants acquire the intended knowledge and skills?	Paper and pencil instruments Simulations Demonstrations Participant reflections Participant portfolios	New knowledge and skills of participants	To improve programme content, format, and organisation
Organisation support and change	Was implementation advocated, facilitated and supported? Was the support public and overt? Were the problems addressed quickly and efficiently? Were sufficient resources made available? What was the impact on the organisation? Did it affect the organisation's climate and procedures?	District (LA) and school records Minutes from follow up meetings Questionnaires Structured interviews with participants and district or school administrators Participant portfolios	The organisation's advocacy, support, accommodation, facilitation, and recognition	To document and improve organisation support To inform future change efforts
Participants' use of new knowledge and skills	Did participants effectively apply the new knowledge and skills?	Questionnaires Structured interviews with participants and their supervisors Participant reflections (oral and/or written) Participant portfolios Direct observations Video or audio tapes	Degree and quality of implementation	To document and improve implementation of programme content
Student learning outcomes	What was the impact on students? Did it affect student performance or achievement? Did it influence students' physical or emotional well-being? Are students more confident as learners? Is student attendance improving? Are dropouts decreasing?	Student records School records Questionnaires Structured interviews with students, parents, teachers and/or administrators Participant portfolios	Student learning outcomes Cognitive (performance and achievement) Affective (attitudes and dispositions) Psychomotor (skills and behaviours)	To focus and improve all aspects of programme design, implementation, and follow up To demonstrate the overall impact of professional development

Guskey suggests that reversing these five levels can be useful in professional development planning:

1. What impact do you want to have on pupils? How will you know that you have had this impact?

2. If that's what you want to accomplish, then what practices do you need to implement it?

3. What does the organisation need to do to support that, e.g. what time/resources do people need?

4. What knowledge do people have to have and what skills do they have to develop?

5. What activities (e.g. training) do people need to gain those skills or knowledge?

We have adapted this idea to include additional levels of impact, as seen in Table 6.4.

Table 6.4 Levels of impact

Level	Measuring
1. Baseline picture	Where you are
2. Goal	Knowing what you want to achieve
3. Plan	Planning the best way
4. The experience	Initial satisfaction with the experience
5. Learning	Knowledge, skills, attitudes acquired or enhanced
6. Organisational support	How the school helps (or hinders) the person using their new learning in their job
7. Into practice	Degree and quality of change (process, product or staff outcome) following from the development activity
8. Pupils' learning outcomes	Impact on experience, attainment and achievement of pupils
9. Other adults in school	Sharing learning with other adults and the impact on them
10. Other pupils	Impact on experience, attainment and achievement of other pupils
11. Adults in other schools	Sharing learning with adults in other schools and the impact on them
12. Pupils in other schools	Impact on experience, attainment and achievement of other pupils

Table 6.5 shows an example of a newly qualified teacher preparing for her first parents' evening and the different levels of impact.

Table 6.5   An example of different levels of impact from one development activity

Level	Measuring
1. Baseline picture	Very apprehensive about my first parents' evening.
2. Goal	To feel confident about parents' evening and for it to go well so that parents are happy and help their children.
3. Plan	Discuss with induction tutor the best way to structure parents' evening. Watch her do one.
4. The experience	The induction tutor's ideas were very helpful. I observed her doing a parent interview. It felt odd at the time but it was useful talking about it afterwards. I noted her body language as well as what she said and how she said it.
5. Learning	Yes, I've got strategies for structuring the interview, keeping to time, having notes and a piece of illustrative work.
6. Organisational support	The SENCO is going to be with me for my first parent interview. I've been given time to make a portfolio of work from my class to illustrate points for parents.
7. Into practice	I carried out interviews at parents' evening confidently and without a hitch.
8. Pupils' learning outcomes	Parents went away with a clear picture of how their children are doing and how to help them. Two pupils have said that they are doing more reading at home.
9. Other adults in school	In the staffroom I told a trainee teacher about my experience and other staff discussed their strategies. Some liked my idea of a portfolio of work.
10. Other pupils	Not sure.
11. Adults in other schools	Yes, I mentioned my learning to another NQT who is going to set up similar structured support in his school. On the new teacher online forum and at the NQT induction programme I shared my strategies for structuring the interview, keeping to time, having notes and a piece of illustrative work. People seemed interested.
12. Pupils in other schools	Too early to say.

What sort of impact are you looking for?

Do you know what sort of impact you are looking for? The TDA funded *Effective Practices in CPD* project looks at impact evaluation in terms of three separate yet related areas – products, processes and outcomes (Earley and Porritt, 2010). Products might include policies or resources. Processes are new or improved systems. But do they really make a difference to staff and children and young people? For example, producing an induction policy for new staff – a product – has the potential to have an impact but it's not what makes the difference per se. Rather, it is how new staff feel about and use it that may make a difference and the outcome would be the difference their feelings or newly developed practice makes on the way they carry out their role and, ultimately, the difference this makes to the learning and experience of the children.

It's useful to consider the different changes we might see in individual members of staff. The impact on individuals' self-esteem is vital. As a teaching assistant said, 'all the CPD at this school has built me up as a person, not just helped me do my job better'. In our research, most support staff said they thought their training and development had at least some impact on their existing skills, new skills and confidence. Approximately two thirds of support staff said their training and development had either 'some' or 'a lot of impact' in these three ways, whilst around a fifth said there was only 'a little' impact (Bubb et al., 2009, p42).

Frost and Durrant (2003) distinguish between three sorts of impact on staff: classroom practice, personal capacity and interpersonal capacity. You might want to see the difference in staff knowledge, behaviours, attitudes, skills and interpersonal capacity as a result of development activities, as seen in Table 6.6.

Table 6.6 Evaluating the impact of training on teaching assistants

Classroom practice	Yes	No	Don't know	N/A
Changes in subject/process knowledge	20	1	2	
Changes in classroom practice	21	1	1	
Personal capacity				
Improved existing skills/practice	21	1	1	
Learned new skills/practice	21	2		
Change in staff confidence and self-esteem	20	2	1	
More positive attitudes/behaviours	17	1	4	1
Happier and more motivated	15	3	3	2
Improved reflection on practice	18	1	4	
Greater ability to take part in/lead change initiatives	20		2	1
Interpersonal capacity				
More effective ways of working together	20	1	1	1
Changes in the practice of colleagues	15	5	3	
More confidence in sharing good practice and managing and influencing colleagues	14	2	3	4
Greater willingness and ability to contribute productively to debate in staff meetings	13	4	1	5
Greater ability to question alternative viewpoints	19		3	1

N = 23

Ultimately, of course, we want to see a difference in the learning and experience of the children – this is what enables us to say that development of staff has been effective. What sort of impact are we looking for in pupils? We can look at their:

- enjoyment in learning
- attitudes
- participation
- pride in and organisation of work

- response to questions and tasks

- performance and progress

- engagement in a wider range of learning activities.

In our research (Bubb et al., 2009, p46) teachers were asked what impact had their training and development in the last 12 months had on pupils. The most popular response was 'better learning' which over half of respondents (55 per cent) selected, followed by 'greater motivation' (38 per cent) and greater confidence (28 per cent). Interestingly, only 15 per cent thought their training and development had resulted in better test results. Several noted the difficulty in quantifying the effect of staff development on pupils' results or outcomes as 'there are too many variables'.

Where to find evidence of impact

Assertions and intentions are useful but staff development leaders need to have evidence of the actual impact of activities. There is much confusion between monitoring and evaluation. Monitoring at the most basic level simply means checking that what has been planned has happened. This can be carried out in a wide range of ways: reminding people, asking for progress reports, and so on. The difficulty lies in finding a system that is manageable, efficient and that works. Perhaps writing progress notes on an action plan about what has been learned will be sufficient. However, measuring someone does not make them grow: it is simply the check that proper nourishment has had its natural effect.

Talking to staff about their development is important, but so is listening to what pupils say. In our research some Year 10 students remembered when lessons were more interactive as a result of staff training on accelerated learning two years before. They thought it was a shame that staff had not kept it up as they thought it helped.

The most common forms of evidence of impact are listed in Table 6.7 where they are divided into qualitative and quantitative sources.

Table 6.7   Sources of evidence of impact

Qualitative	Quantitative
Evaluation after training	Questionnaires – staff
Notes from meetings	Questionnaires – pupils
Discussions – staff and pupils	Test result analysis
Resources, photos, video	Performance data
School improvement partner/external consultant	Analysis of usage e.g. of a VLE
Observation	Pupil tracking records
Pupil work samples	
Performance management reviews	
Departmental reviews	
Self-evaluation forms	
Written reflections/learning journals	

Questionnaires

It is useful to have the same tool to use before and after some development activity. For instance, one school that wanted to improve the confidence and effectiveness of classroom-based support staff designed a questionnaire to judge the present state of affairs, using a Likert scale related to questions such as:

'Have you given teachers any feedback on lessons?'   often / some / a bit / never

The same form was given after training. This information showed who had made progress, to what extent and in what areas.

Questionnaires can be given to different groups (e.g. pupils and teachers; teachers and support staff) to compare responses. You can use open and closed questions, as illustrated in an example from a school which was training sixth formers to help support staff cover lessons (see Table 6.8).

Table 6.8   Questionnaire with open and closed responses (from 11 students)

What did you think of different parts of the programme?

PROGRAMME	Excellent	Good	Satisfactory	Poor
Introduction	3	7	1	0
Behaviour management	5	6	0	0
Starters and plenaries	6	4	1	0
Back-up lessons	2	8	1	0
Overall	5	5	1	0

Once you began work as a cover student, how useful were the training sessions?

Very useful	Of some use	Not much use	No use at all
4	5	1	0

What could be done to improve the training of cover students in the future?

A project trying to raise standards in writing asked teachers to judge whether there had been a positive impact on pupils in specific areas (see Table 6.9).

The discussion around and analysis of this kind of survey is all important. What do you do with the information?

Much impact evaluation can be incorporated into performance management procedures and the school's evaluation of itself. Participants may need time to reflect on what they have learnt and what the impact may be – this could be on their own or with others. Pupil interviews and questionnaires can be very illuminating. Participants can consider questions like these with their line manager, or another identified person such as a mentor or coach:

1. What is your evidence of impact?

2. Does the evidence suggest that the activity had the intended impact on you, your colleagues, your school and your students, when judged against the agreed criteria? If not, why might this be the case?

Table 6.9   Staff views of the impact on pupils as a result of the writing project (from 23 staff)

	Yes	No	Don't know	Not applicable
Enjoyment in learning	22		1	
Participation in learning	23			
Confidence as learners	22		1	
Attitudes towards writing	22			1
Involvement in writing outside lessons	15		6	2
Emotional well-being	18		5	
Performance and progress	23			
Pride in and organisation of work	21		1	1
More effective ways of working	21		1	1
Greater quantity of writing produced	17		3	3
Better quality writing produced	20			3

3. Were there any unexpected outcomes?

4. By considering the impact and its cost, do you think that this activity has been cost-effective?

5. What should you or other key staff do to maximise the impact of this development?

Planning to make a difference

As Guskey says:

> Good evaluation does not need to be complex; what is necessary is good planning and paying attention to evaluation at the outset of the professional development program, not at the end. (Guskey, 2002, p47)

Being clear about exactly what pupil progress you expect as a result of staff development activities is half the battle. Here are two examples:

Example 6.1: Successful planning for impact

A staff development project trying to raise achievement in maths tracked pupil progress in detail so that they were able to say that as a result of the project:

- Pupils are making 1.5–2 sub-levels progress per year across the school (was 1–1.5)

- Lower ability pupils are also making good progress including in Y4 (was a bit flat) so 85 per cent 2b+ mid spring so on track for a level 2a+ by the end of the year and L4+ at the end of KS2

- New arrivals targeted by Learning Guides for pastoral support are settling in well and making good progress – they used to seriously depress our maths results

---

- Embedding new teaching approaches combined with group tuition from the DH has improved attainment in Y5 lower ability set so 80 per cent of cohort now on track for L4+ end of KS2

- Y6 pupils are on track to achieve 86 per cent L4+ and 44 per cent L5+ which is in line with and well above Fisher Family Trust model D targets (so L4+ is in line with progress made by top 25 per cent schools and L5+ in line with progress made by top 10 per cent), and will produce an average point score significantly above national, enabling us to self-evaluate achievement as outstanding (children arrive significantly below national so make outstanding progress)

Example 6.2: Not thinking about impact

A secondary school-wide project on independent learning where teachers were involved in peer observation of new strategies had no clear impact because nothing was done at the outset to plan how to gauge its effectiveness. Attempts to judge the effectiveness of the initiative at its conclusion in relation to its aims were as follows:

- A request for a free text email response from staff to the project manager, supplemented by informal conversations gave positive responses:

  o I try to bring in one of the thinking skills as often as possible

  o It gave me the opportunity to step off the treadmill and think about how I teach

  o I have seen a rapid improvement in the evaluative skills of my Year 10 students. I would generally not expect them all to reach this level until later in the year

- Departmental teams were encouraged to share perceptions gained through the project, but this did not happen in all cases and the results were not collated

- The project manager interviewed some students whose teachers had been involved, but found it difficult to get information that was both useful and reliable

---

In many ways Example 6.2 was a highly successful initiative: the school had managed to complete a complex project involving peer observation and videoing of its teachers. Feedback from teachers showed that it had probably helped to improve practice, but it was unclear in what respects or to what extent. There was no systematic attempt to gauge the impact on the degree of independence demonstrated by students. How outcomes had been improved and the quality of teaching and learning enhanced were not made clear – and the project leaders were not sure what to do next (Bubb and Earley, 2008, pp46–7).

Value for money

With clear evidence of impact, you can look at the value for money and cost-effectiveness of different activities and opportunities. Their cost can be measured in three forms: time, money and disruption to pupils' learning. Certainly, spending vast amounts of money doesn't guarantee great impact; some of the most powerful development happens at comparatively little cost. Looking at cost-effectiveness of

Table 6.10   Cost–benefit analysis of different staff development activities

Activity	Cost	Benefits	Drawbacks	How to maximise efficiency
Course	High	Input from specialists Immerse oneself in the topic Meeting others Sharing ideas Can be inspirational Supporting resources	Expensive Disruptive Cover usually needed May not be good quality Lacks personalisation to needs of individual Inefficient dissemination	Ensure clarity of purpose and impact in advance Possibly more than one person to attend System for dissemination and implementation
Action research	Low	Encourages teamwork and sharing of good practice Sense of working towards a common goal is stimulating	Can be viewed merely as an extension to the 'day job' and not as CPD	Clear focus needs to be established in order to avoid over-generalisation Ground rules to ensure all colleagues make a valid contribution
Teachers TV	Low	Flexible High quality video Discussion of practice Can try out things seen on programmes	Different context Not the complete picture Camera effect	Needs clear focus Time to engage with fully Time to implement

different forms of staff development can be very informative – we must ensure we get good value for money especially when it's in short supply. Table 6.10 gives three examples of staff development activities and builds on the East Midlands CPD Partnership work (www.cpdleader.com) in suggesting a cost–benefit analysis of each, highlighting the drawbacks and ways of maximising efficiency.

Dissemination

Sharing – and sustaining – development is another area that is hard. It is particularly challenging in schools with high staff turnover and poor communication – but even more important. As one headteacher said:

> Staff need to take responsibility for other people's development – organising a staff meeting, ensuring subject knowledge is disseminated, feeding back effectively after a lesson observation – to have an impact on teaching and learning. (Bubb and Earley, 2008, p35)

Staff development leaders need to be creative in designing ways to share, spread and sustain knowledge and skills. Here are some ideas we've come across:

- Staff development planning and evaluation systems ask questions such as, 'How will you share your learning? With whom? When?' (see Table 6.2).

- Information is put into staff bulletins and raised at meetings, twilight training sessions and development days.

- The staff development notice board in the staffroom has an array of useful items and analysis of evaluation forms so that everyone can learn from them.

- The daily briefing meeting is used for people to feed back briefly on any learning they've undertaken or useful TV programmes that are coming up.

- A staff library should contain journals, books and education newspapers and a copy of any materials that anyone on the staff has gained from courses and conferences.

- Send people in pairs or groups to courses in order to aid dissemination.

- Programmes spread over several sessions which have dissemination activities built into them are very useful.

- One school expects staff to write blogs about their development experiences on a section of the intranet. This is very effective in helping staff reflect on their learning and discuss it online, as well as in person. It also has a long shelf-life, often lasting long after the member of staff has left.

- Recognising staff achievement through congratulations at assemblies and staff meetings, and attending award ceremonies not only make the individuals concerned feel good, but also conveys a powerful message to other staff and pupils. One person's effort and achievement often paves the way for others.

We believe that evaluating the impact of staff development is important and that a mature approach to thinking about and understanding the quality of the development of school staff is needed. Without that understanding, staff development will continue to be regarded merely as a series of courses and other occasions or events, rather than as the change, development and improvement of practice for the benefit of learners.

Understanding what staff need in order to develop is essential and it is to this topic that we now turn.

7

How to identify needs

This chapter covers:

- **Procedures**
- **Identifying teachers' needs**
- **Identifying support staff's needs**
- **Individual development plans**

Procedures

In institutions where staff development is most effective, procedures for identifying individual needs, such as performance management (PM) or appraisals, are well thought through and often long-established. All staff believe that this is a way to empower and develop them, rather than a stick with which to beat them. Flexible systems allow for needs to be identified and met as they arise without losing the impetus on original priorities. Connections with school and team development plans are important to make. In most PM systems there is an option for a personal objective in addition to ones designed to meet strategic pupil targets and institutional improvements. In our research we found that staff valued this but did not always set personal objectives because they saw no need for the separation. They felt they had significant input into their objectives and that there was sufficient emphasis on their own development as well as meeting the needs of the school. In one primary, in particular, people felt that their involvement in writing the school improvement plan helped them in identifying professional objectives that contributed to meeting school and pupil needs.

Discovering every individual member of staff's needs is a challenging task. Responsibilities for the identification of staff's needs are usually hierarchically structured (e.g. see Table 7.1) but they needn't be so. Needs identification is often the outcome of a discussion or a debate between the individual staff member and their reviewer or 'line manager'. However, for the workforce as a whole you might also want to consider:

- incorporating a skills check into everyday processes like recruitment and induction

- making a skills check part of your performance management process

- carrying out a full skills audit

- using a training provider to screen staff and assess their skills levels

- using training needs analysis tools.

Table 7.1 An example of who typically identifies whose needs

Member of staff	Appraiser/Reviewer
Headteacher	School improvement partner and governors
Deputy headteacher	Headteacher
Assistant headteachers	Deputy headteacher
Teachers	Assistant headteachers
Senior teaching assistant	Deputy headteacher
Teaching assistants	Senior teaching assistant
Head of extended services	Deputy headteacher
Site manager	Headteacher
Administrative manager	Headteacher
Kitchen assistants	Head of catering
Cleaning staff	Site manager
Domestic staff	Site manager
Administrative staff	Administrative manager

Many schools use audits to find out what skills and experience staff have and need. The online audit offered by the National Association of Professional Teaching Assistants (NAPTA) is popular. This gives a detailed profile of the person in terms of their current qualifications and professional strengths.

Meetings to identify needs and plan how to meet them take between about 30 minutes and an hour, if they are taken seriously. The discussion should be guided by questions that seek to identify strengths as well as areas for development and career plans. Here are two schools' sets of questions which they use as a structure:

School A:

1. What we like and admire about you

2. What's important now?

3. What's important for the future?

4. What's working?

5. What's not working?

6. What support is needed to keep your professional development healthy?

School B:

1. What are the aspects of your current role you feel have been particularly successful?

2. Are there any aspects of your role where you feel you have been less successful?

3. Have there been any obstacles/problems/difficulties which have prevented you from achieving any of your goals?

4. How do you think these might be overcome?

5. Have you any skills or abilities which you feel are not being used to advantage within the school?

This last question is an important one. Too few organisations know what skills and interests their workforce possesses. Who knows how they might be used to help pupils or give an extra dimension to staff relationships? For instance, a TA was learning British Sign Language in her own time and then started teaching it to pupils as a club. In another school, a disparate group of individuals with a range of roles from across the organisation found a shared interest in gardening that motivated all of them. They swapped tips, seeds, plants and produce and set up a gardening club with pupils and cultivated several patches of the school grounds.

Some organisations use 360 degree feedback with comments from up to six people to achieve a detailed picture of an individual. This is highly celebratory and does much to motivate because a summary (such as shown in Table 7.2) is shared with the individual and then married up with the self-evaluation before deciding on new objectives.

Table 7.2   360 Feedback

What six people who work with, under and above you say are your strengths:

- Organised amazingly well, not stinting on hard work
- Showed leadership especially in standing up in front of large groups
- Very good with organising masses of students – good management
- She's real – there's no phoniness whatsoever. She's not reserved at all, which is great
- Working with her has probably been one of the most pleasurable experiences since I've been here
- She loves what she does and is great at it
- She provides support, encouragement, practical help. She's amazing
- It feels good to know that X is so organised, which means that nothing is left until the last minute which avoids stress
- She knows the syllabus inside and out so I have faith that when I have a problem I can go to her for help
- She is willing to share resources and always offers help
- I think she's been tenacious in fighting for funds and equipment in the face of whatever obstacle
- She does everything possible in order to help the students achieve their potential

What people say are areas for you to develop:

- Don't get too tired or she'll wear herself out
- Needs to relax sometimes, to step back and take time to breathe. Part of the problem is that she doesn't have the support she needs
- Be aware of whole-school pressures and issues and how her actions might impact on other departments and developments

Identifying teachers' needs

Induction and performance management should help identify teachers' needs, but does it? The *Staff Development Outcomes Study* (Bubb et al., 2009) found that performance management was generally going well. In its national survey, around half of senior staff and teachers considered PM 'useful' and around one fifth 'very useful' for their career development, skills development, ability to do the job better, and in boosting self-esteem. However, up to a quarter of teachers and senior staff considered that PM was 'not useful'. The *State of the Nation* research concluded that 'It was usually happenchance if CPD arose out of a PM interview: CPD outcomes were seen as very fragmented and ad hoc and there was no expectation that discussion about this would be part of the process' (Storey et al., 2008, p32).

The TDA *Framework of Teacher Standards* (www.tda.gov.uk/standards) can provide a useful platform from which to discuss needs. However the findings from research suggest that:

- use is limited because not everyone has heard of the *Framework*

- those who have used it, value it

- senior staff use, or say they use, the standards more than classroom teachers

- the standards are seen more as a means of supporting PM than to aid forward planning such as identifying development needs or career planning.

It is clear that there is a significant number of teachers who are unaware of the *Framework of Teacher Standards*. This is of concern given the central importance of the standards in career progression and pay.

Activity: Watch *Performance Management – A Fresh Approach*
www.teachers.tv/video/25568

What do you think of this school's approach to PM?

Could their professional learning journal work for you?

There will be a range of teachers in any school. The VITAE project (Day et al., 2006) found that teachers do not necessarily become more effective with experience. Indeed, teachers in later years are at greater risk of becoming less effective, particular those with 24–30 years of experience. The project identified six professional life phases within which there were people who were feeling positive or negative, as seen in the percentages below. Recognising the impact of influences in particular professional life phases and providing informal and formal development and support are key means of building and sustaining teacher commitment and effectiveness.

Professional life phases, from the VITAE project (Day, 2008)

Professional life phase 0–3 years: Commitment, support and challenge

a) developing sense of efficacy (60%)

b) reducing sense of efficacy (40%).

Professional life phase 4–7 years: Identity and efficacy in classroom

a) sustaining a strong sense of identity, self-efficacy and effectiveness (49%)

b) sustaining identity, efficacy and effectiveness (31%)

c) identity, efficacy and effectiveness at risk (20%).

Professional life phase 8–15 years: Managing changes in role and identity: growing tensions and transitions

a) sustained engagement (76%)

b) detachment/loss of motivation (24%).

Professional life phase 16–23 years: Work–life tension, challenges to motivation and commitment

a) further career advancement and good results have led to increased motivation/ commitment (52%)

b) sustained motivation, commitment and effectiveness (34%)

c) workload/managing competing tension/career stagnation have led to decreased motivation, commitment and effectiveness (14%).

Professional life phase 24–30 years: Challenges to sustaining motivation

a) sustained a strong sense of motivation and commitment (54%)

b) holding on but losing motivation (46%).

Professional life phase 31+ years: Sustaining/declining motivation, ability to cope with change, looking to retire

a) maintaining commitment (64%)

b) tired and trapped (36%).

The VITAE project identified influences which affect teachers' sense of effectiveness across all phases:

a) personal life experiences/events

b) school (roles and responsibilities, classroom settings, leadership and colleagues)

c) pupils (relationships and behaviour)

d)   professional values

e)   policies.

This is likely to be true for support staff too. The researchers found that teachers who work in schools in challenging circumstances face persistent challenges of managing pupil behaviour and maintaining health. Many teachers in the 8–15 years phase of their career face increasing work–life management tensions which may adversely affect their commitment and effectiveness. These teachers are likely to need help sustaining commitment and quality in the context of the management of the more complex roles which many are now taking. Day says:

> Creating positive work conditions, meeting teachers' professional and personal needs and minimising teacher burnout are key to encouraging teachers' resilience, promoting teacher wellbeing and positive professional life trajectories, improving the conditions for teachers' effectiveness in relation to pupils' performance and, ultimately, school improvement. They are key tasks for school leaders. (Day, 2008)

Key tasks, indeed, for school leaders, especially those who are leading staff development. Workload and stress are significant reasons for leaving teaching and schools facing challenging circumstances are the worst affected, and it is here the notion of resilience is likely to be most significant. Additional support too is important in such schools and is more likely to be successful in recruiting and retaining staff than financial inducements.

Sometimes it takes another person to identify someone's needs. New teachers, for instance, benefit from an induction tutor who can help them see the wood from the trees. Too often new teachers are said to need help with managing behaviour but addressing time management can be very effective. A second year teacher in looking back at his first year realised the impact that ineffectual time management outside of lessons can have on student behaviour within them. He said:

> Preparing lesson resources on a Monday morning rather than a Friday evening gave me a start to the week that was far more stressful than necessary ... The obvious result of my mistakes was that I felt over-burdened and less prepared in my teaching – increasing the chances of behavioural incidents. Suddenly the time-management dilemma was accentuated, because now the hour during which I would have planned next week's lessons was spent contacting parents, writing up incident reports or talking with heads of year. (Izzett, 2009, p9)

It is clear that teachers who are in different professional life phases, in different schools and experiencing different working conditions, will not have the same needs, and that in each of these circumstances there will be those whose commitment and capacity for effectiveness will be in danger of being compromised. This may apply especially to those in the middle and later years and those who work in schools in challenging circumstances.

It is equally clear that the needs of these groups of teachers 'will be met best through interaction with leaders in schools who have a close knowledge of staff, who engage in high levels of interaction, who nurture trust and respect and who themselves are committed to lifelong learning' (Day, 2008).

Identifying support staff needs

The survey for the *Staff Development Outcomes Study* (Bubb et al., 2009) found that seven out of ten support staff were included in some sort of performance management or appraisal and that they found this useful. However, 9 per cent of support staff said that their needs were not identified. The *Support Staff* research project (Teeman et al., 2008) found the same: 76 per cent said that there were systems to help them identify needs but 'just under a tenth of support staff said that no-one helped them to identify their training and development needs'. Of the 38 Testbed schools (Coldwell et al., 2008) that had a performance review system in place, 22 included all staff in the system, 11 involved just teachers and five involved just teachers and teaching assistants. In all but one training and development were linked to performance reviews.

In the *Staff Development Outcomes Study* (Bubb et al., 2009) case study schools with strongest staff development, much effort was put into identifying the needs of support staff, based on an understanding of opportunities and career frameworks. The *CPD Leadership* research (Robinson et al., 2008) found that a range of people led support staff development but that technicians, library staff, catering staff, people dedicated to extended services provision and volunteers were the least likely to have anyone taking responsibility for identifying their needs.

The national occupational standards (NOS) can be very useful. Found at www. tda.gov.uk/nos, these are statements of performance that describe what support staff need to do, know and understand in their role. For example, a teaching assistant can demonstrate that they meet the standards relating to supporting pupils' learning through evidence of their work, regardless of their subject specialism. The NOS standards can help support staff:

- define the coverage and focus of their role

- assess how well they are performing

- identify training and development needs

- select qualifications that match their role

- make the links with the school's overall aims and objectives.

The standards support national vocational qualifications (NVQs) and can be used to develop other qualifications.
Each NOS unit follows a similar structure, such as this:

National occupational standard: Supporting teaching and learning in schools STL16: provide displays (IL3/10)

Who is this unit for?

This unit is for those who set up, maintain and dismantle displays. In the context of a school the displays will generally be designed to support teaching and learning and/or celebrate achievement.

What is this unit about?

This unit is about setting up and removing displays. It involves identifying the purpose of the display, designing the display, deciding what it will contain, and gathering together materials for the display. It also covers ensuring the display is safe, keeping it tidy and removing the display when it is no longer required. In schools, the teacher would advise on the purpose, content and nature of displays and pupils will be active participants in providing materials for display.

16.1 set up displays performance criteria

You need to:

1. Identify the purpose of the display clearly

2. Devise the design and content of the display to maintain an appropriate balance between effective visual presentation and security of material

3. Obtain and create material and equipment for the display

4. Locate the display in an appropriate and accessible place for users

5. Display all relevant material

6. Ensure that the display is stable and safe

7. Determine the optimum time duration for the display, by reference to its theme, purpose and materials used.

Place in qualifications

This unit is an optional unit in both the level 2 and level 3 NVQ/SVQ in supporting teaching and learning in schools.

Individual development plans

Systems help identify why meeting certain needs are important and what the outcome will be. When discussing areas for development think about identifying where a person is on a ten point scale in relation to the specific issue and what a realistic goal is, as shown in Figure 7.1. This stops people aiming for perfection and gives them a specific target because they will describe what they're doing that makes it a three, rather than a two or four and what being at six on the scale will look like.

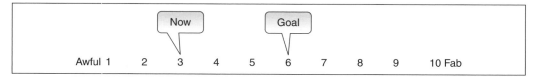

Figure 7.1   Goals – where do I want to be?

Table 7.3   Individual development plan A

| *What are my learning needs and personal goals?* |
| To raise the profile of art across the school, ensuring that teachers effectively manage the demands of the curriculum by making appropriate links with other subject areas. |
| To be more confident in undertaking classroom observations. |
| To develop a strategic overview of a whole subject across a creative curriculum. |

| *What has led me to identify this need?* |
| Discussions with SMT. Performance management target to develop my role. |

What are my objectives in meeting this need?

- Ensure the scheme of work is being used effectively across each key stage.
- Ensure teachers' planning shows clear cross-curricular links.
- Evidence of the subject being valued – shown in time dedicated in weekly planning and displays.
- To ensure we are working with a similar structure of art lessons to provide consistency across the area of learning.
- To supply teachers with resources, objectives and planning.
- To team teach to model an art lesson.

How will I meet these objectives?

Key Actions	Timescale	Resources/Personnel	Success Criteria
Discussion in staff meeting – letting the team know my action plan. Questionnaire to find out teachers' thoughts on art and planning.	Week 1	Action Plan. Questionnaire.	To identify two teachers to work with on their unit of art for the summer term. To find out teachers' thoughts on planning and what are they using to support their teaching of art.
Meeting with the two teachers identified to discuss their art unit and main topic.	Week 2	Curriculum map. Print out of units. Thought shower of ideas to share with teacher. Discuss their confidence with teaching art.	Identify a link with a topic.
To plan out a unit of work (with teacher input).	Week 3	QCA unit of work. Ideas attached to the unit. Examples of resources to use with the units. Teachers' thoughts.	To have a planned unit of work linked with a topic area. To arrange team teaching the first session to model to the teacher.
To discuss and feedback about how the unit is going.	Week 4	Talk time with teacher. Key questions to ask and have verbal response.	Reflect on the thoughts of the teacher. Arrange a lesson observation.
To observe the teachers. To fill out questionnaire by teacher and pupils.	Week 5	Lesson observations. Questionnaires for teachers and pupils.	To have given written feedback. To have the thoughts of pupils and teacher and how they found the unit.
To share their art learning in assembly.	Week 7	Video and photos.	To share what they have achieved as a class. Teachers to recognise the outcome.

Key Actions	Timescale	Resources/Personnel	Success Criteria
			Celebrate art across the school. To have videoed some art.
To arrange a staff meeting on modelling an art lesson.	To be arranged	SMT to agree.	Confidence in teaching art across the school.

Who can support me in achieving this and how?
Teachers – willing to share good practice, planning as well as identifying areas they feel they need to build confidence in, so that training can be given in these areas.
SMT – time to assess the value of the subject across the school.
Pupils – share their experiences of art through pupil questionnaire.

How will I evaluate my learning?
I intend to interview staff to elicit their thoughts on developments to date.

How will I share my learning?
Presentation to the staff team.
In assembly with the two classes in question.
Photographic evidence will be produced alongside video recording.
I will also share my learning with other colleagues on the leadership course I am currently attending.

Table 7.4 Individual development plan B (from: South Yorkshire LEAs – CPD Tool Kit – 3.4. Individual CPD Plan)

Name: Annie Dale			Role: Classroom Teacher, History Co-ordinator	
	Outcomes – pupils and staff	**Effect on myself**	**Learning Activities**	**Resources**
Development linked to school development priorities	Raise standards in writing	Increase knowledge, skills and understanding Build self-confidence	Observe X modelling shared writing Discuss planning with co-ordinator	30 mins cover + 20 mins 20 mins
Development to enhance skills for current job	Develop continuity and progression in History throughout school	Develop new role as History Co-ordinator	Coaching in leadership role Coaching from an experienced co-ordinator Attend LA Co-ordinator meetings	2 – ½ days £175 2 – ½ day visits £300 2 twilights
Development linked to professional aspirations	Increased effectiveness in shared writing and subject co-ordination	See above	Take advantage of coaching opportunities and peer observation	
Cover Fee £	Course Fee £	Travel Costs £	Total £	
Plan created and agreed between...and... (Team Leader) Date.......................... (A copy to Professional Portfolio and Headteacher)				

An individual development plan – sometimes called personal learning or training plans – may include some or all of these elements, as the examples in Tables 7.3 and 7.4 show:

- evaluation of strengths and weaknesses

- targets and objectives and how these will be achieved

- timescales for achieving targets

- resource implications, such as cost and time

- arrangements for regular review and evaluation and minutes of review meetings

- a record of development activities to date

- details of responsibility areas and current job description

- identification of gaps in training and development, including a comparison of a precise job description with existing expertise, and training planned.

8

How to personalise learning

This chapter covers:

- **What we know**
- **How adults learn**
- **Approaches to personalising development**

What we know

There is much discussion about personalising the learning experience for students but we need to think about similar processes and practices for the workforce – for adult as well as young learners. We saw in Chapter 1 (Activity) how one school personalises development programmes for all their staff and three discuss their development journeys: from PE teacher to assistant principal, TA to teacher and from nurse to school nurse. All staff have training and development needs and organisations will set up various systems to identify them (see Chapter 7). Individual needs can be divided into professional, personal and a mixture of the two, pro-personal needs – the personal development required to meet professional needs, such as resilience.

Ofsted (2006) and others have noted how in recent years the focus has been on organisational priorities and that planning for individuals' needs, where not clearly linked to the former, has been weak. However, the success of any plans and priorities will ultimately depend on improving the quality of the workforce, especially the quality of teaching and learning. Educational improvements will only come about by focusing on the development of our 'human resources'. So individual and school needs have to be brought together and managed within an existing budget. Fortunately they often go together but organisations that ignore the individual needs of their staff do so at their own peril!

From the staff development leader's perspective meeting the needs of individuals requires much thought and careful planning. The school workforce is now made up of many roles, in fact in some places teaching staff may be in a minority. Each person will have different needs, different preferences for learning (or learning styles), be at different stages of development and at different stages of their career. No wonder there has been a tendency to provide a 'one size fits all' approach to staff development! Personalising individual staff development is not easy but it has to be considered if the most is to be gained from the opportunities made available. How well do you and others know your staff and what their individual needs and preferences are? Staff development has the potential to motivate, refresh and above all to help people get better at what they do. This is more likely if individuals feel that their needs (and wants) are being catered for. One of the problems, for example, with development days, as we show in Chapter 5, is that people often feel their needs are not being met – what Cordingley calls 'one size fits no-one INSET days' (2008b).

The most effective types of staff development are perceived to be those that directly meet individual needs. Research has found that teachers expressed high levels of dissatisfaction with development events that did not meet their needs or failed to live up to their expectations. There was, however, also a recognition that staff development had to meet a variety of needs and not only their own as individuals. The forms of development that were said by teachers to be most effective and considered to have the greatest impact on professional growth and change were observation and professional discussion (Goodall et al., 2005).

A growing body of research tells us that the kinds of staff development which make the most difference are based on dialogue about teaching and learning and the improvement of practice through a variety of activities including coaching, mentoring, shadowing and peer support. Awareness-raising events are useful for absorbing information and updating knowledge but are not likely to lead to skills development. Joyce and Showers (2002) concluded that, for training to be truly effective, it needs to include the following five components or stages:

- theory – where the new approach is explained and justified

- demonstration – to give a model of how this can be put into practice

- practice – so that the staff member can try out the new approach

- feedback on how well the new approach is working

- coaching – to help the staff member discuss the teaching and learning in a supportive environment and consider how it might be improved.

Their research showed that, without the opportunity to receive feedback and coaching, there is no measurable impact on classroom practice. However, once these two components are added, in particular the final coaching stage, there is a large and measurable impact on practice.

So, although we can make some general statements about what works and what doesn't – we have a growing knowledge base about effective forms of development – less is known about staff learning. We know, for example, that we do not all learn in the same way. Is adult learning the same or different, for example, from pupil learning? Will a better understanding of how adults learn enable us to personalise staff development or at least ensure we are catering for their different learning styles? If we wish staff development to lead to improved practice and enhanced student outcomes then a better understanding of how adults learn is needed.

We need to give thought to the forms or methods of development and recognise that individuals will have preferred learning approaches. For example the CfBT/Lincs (2007) resource pack notes how needs identification should link to value-for-money methods, firstly, by raising awareness of the cost of different types of provision and, secondly, by asking if the method is personalised to the preferred learning approach of the individual being trained. Members of the school workforce can be asked to show their preferences for different types or forms of development (e.g. critical friendship groups, school visits, job rotation, exchanges or placements) to ensure, costs permitting, that these match their preferred learning methods (adult personalisation or individualised learning). What are your and your staff's preferred learning methods?

How adults learn

There's been lots of debate about children's learning styles but not much on how to help the adults in schools to learn. Do you know how you learn best? Do you know how the site manager or catering manager learn best? If you're going to help staff make the most of development opportunities, these are important questions because there are many ways to achieve the same end. Thinking about 'andragogy' (how adults learn) is important because, for instance, we know that adults learn best when the topic is of immediate use.

We also know that adult learners:

- will commit to learning when they believe that the objectives are realistic and important for their personal and professional needs

- want to be responsible for their own learning and should therefore have some control over the what, who, how, why, when, and where of their learning

- need direct, concrete experiences for applying what they have learned to their work

- do not automatically transfer learning into daily practice and often benefit from coaching and other kinds of follow-up support to sustain learning

- need feedback on the results of their efforts

- come to the learning process with self-direction and a wide range of previous experiences, knowledge, interests, and competencies. (Speck and Knipe, 2005)

Some people consider that adults have preferred learning styles. For instance, Honey and Mumford (www.peterhoney.com) identify four different types of adult learners: theorists, pragmatists, activists and reflectors.

- Theorists like to learn in structured situations where they're offered interesting ideas and concepts, such as lectures, deep discussions, reading and thinking alone. They learn less when they have to participate in situations that emphasise emotions.

- Pragmatists learn best when the topic is of obvious relevance and when shown something they can put into practice. They learn less well when there's no practice or guidelines as to how something is done.

- Activists learn best when involved in new experiences, problem-solving, team tasks and role-play. They learn less well when listening to lectures or long explanations; reading, writing, or thinking on their own; absorbing data; or following instructions to the letter.

- Reflectors like time to think about the subject such as through lectures with plenty of reflection time; observation; and keeping a learning log/journal to review what has happened. They learn less when role-playing, being thrown in at the deep end or worried by deadlines.

Few people fall neatly into one category, but have a leaning towards one or two. Honey and Mumford's questionnaire aims to help people pinpoint their learning preferences so that they're in a better position to select learning experiences that suit them or understand that they need to work harder in some types of development activity.

Experiential learning

Experiential learning is important for adults as well as pupils. Development programmes that make use of action and experiential learning principles have been found to have greater impact. They make the learning process 'real' and encourage learners to take responsibility for planning and implementing their own learning experiences to meet their needs.

The experiential learning cycle of 'do, review, learn and apply' (Dennison and Kirk, 1990) is well known. So, someone who wants to get better at being on the school reception desk, for instance, might usefully go through the cycle in this way:

Do	Observe someone that I admire work on the school reception desk
Review	Think about it and discuss it with them afterwards
Learn	Learn some key techniques for being the public face or voice of the school
Apply	Try them out when I'm on duty on reception
Do	Get someone to observe me dealing with parents and give me feedback.

People learn in different ways and have preferred learning styles but learning takes place in a variety of ways and in different settings. It can be formal or informal, within the workplace or off-site. You can think of learning in vertical dimensions (knowing more, new learning and experiences) and horizontal ones (the same knowledge applied in different contexts, deeper understanding). So, people don't always have to learn new things to be developing, but at some level they will be changing their practice.

Managing change

Change is hard: many factors are involved. For a greater chance of success there needs to be a recognition that something needs to be better, an aim, the expertise to make the improvement, the motivation to do so, help from others, a plan of action and time. If any one of these factors is missing, people will find it hard to develop.

Let's think about Maggie who is a member of the support staff with responsibility for a tutor group. There is low level poor behaviour in registration and form time. The chatting and mucking about are getting her down. So she needs:

- Recognition that something needs to be better

- Aim – knowing how she wants her tutor group to behave

- Expertise – she has behaviour management skills that she uses successfully when in the role of a teaching assistant

- Motivation – people have complained about the noise the tutor group makes

- Help – advice from colleagues; observation of other tutor groups; reading articles; time to think through what she's going to do

- Plan – drawing up a plan of what she's going to do and when

- Time – the time to think things through, gain help and put new strategies into practice.

If she doesn't recognise that things need to improve nothing will change. Without an aim or vision of how she wants them to behave, she won't develop because she doesn't know what her boundaries for behaviour are. Without the expertise to improve behaviour, such as rewards and sanctions, she'll get anxious and feel inadequate. If there is no motivation, like people complaining or someone observing her, she may develop but not quickly. She'll get frustrated if there is no help, such as advice from colleagues, books to read, observation of other people's tutor groups, or time to think through what she's going to do. Without a plan, written or mental, she may not get round to improving things consistently. If she has no time to think things through, gain help and put new strategies into practice then nothing will change.

Approaches to personalising development

A personalised approach which can be used across the whole school workforce and which tries to link individual and institutional needs is The Expert Trail.

An approach to personalising staff development – The Expert Trail

The Expert Trail (www.realtrust.org.uk) is an approach to staff development whereby all staff have the opportunity to undertake a five stage self-directed process of training and development that is linked in some way to improving the teaching and learning in the school and thereby raising achievement. Individual staff are given a 'treasury' of time (two half days + three INSET afternoons per year) to undertake their development. A professional studies manager gives support and reviews progress. The headteacher celebrates successes with the individual, who is given a small honorarium and gives a presentation to the rest of the staff.

(Continued)

(Continued)

A headteacher from one of our research schools said:

> After 17 months the scheme has already unleashed a torrent of enthusiasm and revealed a range of talents that the school did not know about. The biggest impact has been on the teaching assistants but many staff welcome the time to develop their own thing. The impact on the children's learning has been there for all to see. Vulnerable children have achieved more, our Gifted and Talented programme is effective in raising our Level 5 teacher assessment scores in writing and the number of out of hours clubs has doubled to over 30 resulting in more vulnerable children attending and achieving more in class.

Some schools ask staff to keep a learning log or a causation trail, to help them keep track of cause and effect. One school we visited for our research asks its staff to keep a diary, which teachers write fortnightly and TAs weekly. As well as writing how pupils are doing, staff write about how they are implementing their own learning from development activities and the difference this is making to the children. This is a valuable way to see what is working, and means that training needs can be met very quickly, and for the benefit of children. All staff seemed happy to write it and enjoyed both the process and the dialogue it engendered with the head and deputy who not only read, but wrote comments on them as formative feedback.

Activity: Watch the following videos using Teachers TV, Learning journey for governors

1. Just for New Governors – Know your Role www.teachers.tv/video/4881

This seems like an essential first port of call for anyone wanting to get involved in governorship. Keeping abreast of what it means to be a governor and understanding the many challenges of the role are vital.

2. School Matters – Every Child Matters – A Healthcheck www.teachers. tv/video/22378

Governors also need to keep abreast of the key issues in education. This programme should enable them to develop a greater understanding of the Every Child Matters agenda, which will inform their strategic thinking and planning for their school.

3. Gifted and Talented – A Whole School www.teachers.tv/video/28717

This programme deals with a whole school issue that is particularly relevant, as governors have a watching brief on pupils' achievement in their school.

4. The Jonathan Dimbleby Big Debate – The Poverty Gap www.teachers.tv/video/22604

This programme, which is part of a series, should offer another great means for governors to keep up to date with current affairs in an engaging and informative way.

5. Just for Governors – Child Protection www.teachers.tv/video/2867

The responsibilities of the governing body in relation to child protection are clearly an important issue. Hopefully this programme will provide access to the information needed.

What kind of learning journey do you think a person who watched theses videos would experience? What are the next steps they should take?

(www.teachers.tv/learningjourneys)

Keeping a development portfolio

Everyone needs somewhere to keep all their development related paperwork. Some people keep portfolios electronically, using software such as Sims or Blue. A development portfolio should be where staff keep all their objectives, action plans, reflections and assessments for their whole career and be used for induction, performance management, promotion and job applications. It shouldn't be onerous to keep. If any parts of a portfolio don't work, encourage people to change them – it's theirs!

Here's how the contents could be organised:

The Development Portfolio

1. Career history

    • CV and qualifications

    • References

    • Job descriptions

2. Objectives

    • Objectives

    • Action plans

3. Development activities

    • Development activities and meetings

    • Handouts

    • Certificates

    • Notes from observing other staff

    (Continued)

(Continued)

- Articles read and websites visited
- List of networks made

4. Evidence of effectiveness

- Performance management
- Monitoring
- Evidence of standards

5. Other information

- Policies for induction, staff development and performance management
- Information about people who can help

Personalising individual staff development is important but it does present a challenge and has to be considered if the most is to be gained from the opportunities made available. But what opportunities are there for staff development other than going on courses? It is to the question of how to meet staff's needs that we now turn.

9

How to meet staff's needs

This chapter covers:

- **What we know**
- **The range of activities**

  - o **Research and enquiry**
  - o **Coaching-mentoring**
  - o **Observation**
  - o **Teachers TV**
  - o **Reading**
  - o **E-communities**
  - o **Listening to pupils**
  - o **Training others**

Once the needs of staff have been identified, the next stage in the training and development cycle is to plan a range of relevant activities and opportunities to meet them. This is a challenge because individuals' needs have to be considered whilst addressing the institutional and collective needs reflected in school improvement and development plans.

What we know

Where needs were met well in our research on outstanding schools, staff felt that they were able to access training and development activities that were appropriate to their needs, life, and learning styles, whether this was through formal training or in an on-the-job, informal way. Most considered that their schools offered a wide range of opportunities, including professional dialogue, peer mentoring and action research as well as external and in-school training sessions. Few people used reading or watching Teachers TV programmes to help them develop: support staff were more likely to do so than teachers. At some schools the personal interests and 'natural talents/interests' of staff were encouraged and developed. One primary headteacher encouraged staff to pursue 'personal entitlements' which he was prepared to finance at up to £200 per person. Activities included learning to play a musical instrument, hill walking, buying and using a digital camera and attending conferences. This was to make staff 'feel good', motivating them to undertake their professional duties.

Senior leaders identified a wide variety of development activities that seemed to have an impact on staff, and then on pupils. Projects and courses spanning a term or more, with activities to trial or research and involving purposeful collaboration, were what seemed to make most impact overall on school improvement. Also cited were:

- formal training

- working with people in their own and other schools

- working with people from outside the school

- having time to think about and plan how to implement new skills

- receiving advice and support from other staff

- running and leading training

- discussing in team meetings and being able to contribute ideas

- coaching and mentoring

- observing others and being observed (Bubb et al., 2009, p29).

The *State of the Nation* survey (McCormick et al., 2008) found that teachers participated in a wide range of development activities but the most common were:

- in-school workshops (77 per cent)

- out-of-school workshops (60 per cent)

- mentoring or related activities (52 per cent).

Few participated in university courses (7 per cent), in teacher study groups (12 per cent) or in non-university accredited courses (14 per cent).

Senior staff considered that networks and coaching and mentoring (see Figure 9.1) were the activities that had been most useful to them in terms of their development as a leader. Advanced Skills Teachers valued working with other ASTs across the country.

Where needs are not met well

Our research has found that where needs were not met well there was too much emphasis on courses and too little on other forms of staff development. Hindrances or barriers to meeting development needs often centred around working hours and affected part-timers rather than full-timers, and support staff rather than teachers.

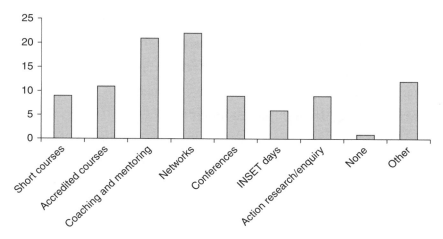

Figure 9.1   Activities most useful for leadership development in the last 12 months (%) (Bubb et al., 2009, p27)

Where support staff were negative, it was because they felt that they had few training and development opportunities. There were five main reasons for this:

- financial constraints in which they felt they were at the bottom of priorities

- lack of time

- poor or non-existent performance management systems

- contractual issues such as only being paid for the pupil day

- not being valued.

An example of the last point was where a premises officer's request for the school to contribute to the completion of his electrician's qualification was turned down. He felt that senior staff did not trust or value him, even though having the qualification would save the school a great deal of time and money because he could do the work instead of contractors.

Many teaching and special needs assistants are only employed for specific hours within the school day, which means that they miss out on after-school training and development. Some schools solved this by paying people extra, giving time off in lieu or by running TA training within the school day.

What we know works

Based on our research and experience we believe that development activities are likely to be more effective if participants:

- choose them to fit in with their life, work and timelines

- see their relevance

- want to do them

- understand the intended outcomes

- are involved from the outset in evaluating their impact
- feel that their existing knowledge and expertise are taken into account
- appreciate the teaching and learning strategies employed
- have opportunities to apply what they have learned
- are open to learning beyond that intended.

Development that comes from a range of formal and informal blended learning activities is likely to be most effective in making a difference.

The range of activities

The range of staff development activities is wide and includes off-the-job, on-the-job and close-to-the-job opportunities. These can be categorised into four overlapping groups: individual; within school; cross-school networks; and external.

The range of development activities

Individual – thinking; reading books, periodicals and the educational press; research and enquiry; self-study; watching programmes on Teachers TV; keeping a learning log or reflective diary.

Within school – working with others; talking to other staff (peers and those with expertise); coaching/mentoring; development days; staff/team meetings; being observed; discussing a lesson; observing; collaborative planning; team teaching; listening to pupils' views; observing some learners; tracking a pupil; action research groups; trying things out and doing things differently; taking on a new role; shadowing colleagues, training others; attending governing body meetings; chairing a meeting; leading working groups; attachments to the senior team, etc.

Cross-school networks – formal and informal networks; training; visiting other schools, similar to or different from yours; reading and talking to others on on-line communities e.g. National College's Talk2learn or the TES online staffroom; working with people, such as ASTs, from other schools; networks of local schools or ones set up for a specific project; developing people from other schools.

External expertise – one day events; longer courses; blended learning programmes that involve some external expertise and school-based activity; conferences; working with community groups, consultants, local authorities, universities, government agencies or subject associations.

The most successful learning is likely to involve activities from several or all of the above groups, but many adults in schools say they learn best through on-the-job training and applying skills in real life situations – from the workplace more than the workshop.

You could ask your staff what's best for them. In our own research one primary school used free online audits to gauge how teachers and support staff felt about

Table 9.1   Which kind of development is most useful? (Bubb and Earley, 2008, p32)

	Teachers (n = 19)	Support staff (n = 18)
Most useful	Lesson observations School-based training 1:1 coaching External INSET	1:1 coaching School-based training Lesson observations External INSET
Least useful	Reading and web research	Reading and web research

the different types of development they had experienced. It was quick and easy for people to do and the data were analysed simply, as can be seen in Table 9.1. The findings from the audits were used to provide more of the types of development which people felt most useful and thus provided good value for money.

It is not possible for us to give consideration to all of the staff development activities in the above four groups but we'd like to examine a few in more detail, namely research and enquiry; coaching-mentoring; observation; Teachers TV; reading; e-communities; listening to pupils; and training others.

Research and enquiry

Are your staff keen to reflect upon their work, explore different approaches, and try out new things in the classroom? One of the reasons why undertaking research and enquiry is such a powerful development tool is that it is appropriate to the needs of adult learners. Members of staff undertaking research and enquiry, especially when working collaboratively, make a very powerful brew. But what do we mean by research and enquiry? It involves reflecting on your own practice, individually and collectively, finding out more, gaining new insights and making changes as a result. All members of the workforce can get involved in research and enquiry although it has been dominated by teachers. Schools and colleges that are enquiry driven are often referred to as 'research-engaged', 'self-evaluative', 'reflective', 'thinking', 'learning organisations' or 'learning-centred'. How would you describe yours? Would any of these labels apply?

 Activity: Watch *School Matters – action research* www.teachers. tv/video/4883

Look at three schools' approaches to action research in addressing:

- managing a high level of newly arrived children
- improving reading at key stage 1
- improving boys' performance at *GCSE* level.

How could you use these examples in your setting?

Accredited courses often have a research element. Although research projects are undertaken by individuals, the impact can benefit many staff. As part of his research for a Masters degree, a teacher examined the impact of different elements of the 'Learning to Learn' programme on the early career teachers at his school. He said:

> My research has made a difference to the way we do things at school. I found that staff really value discussing issues formally and informally so we've tried to build in collaboration as a key part of staff development. Now, the sessions we run are much more focused on working together. (Holbrook, 2009, p11)

Some organisations link up with a university to provide Masters modules based at school. A school that wanted to encourage research and reflection amongst its staff, beginning with teachers in their early years and extending it to support staff, was prepared to fund accredited programmes as seen in case study 9.1.

 Case study 9.1: *School-based Masters programme* (based on www.teachers.tv/video/28595/resources)

A London secondary school is using a MA programme to enhance individual development, foster an action research culture and drive aspects of school improvement. The first group of seven researched aspects of the school development plan, with significant impact:

> The introduction of vocational courses – led to tasters in Year 9
> Use of ALIS data for sixth form – led to introduction and training for staff
> Rewards for KS4 students – to be included in revised behaviour policy
> Expansion of community languages – to include Asset Languages
> Use of student observers and co-coaching – became established practice
> Environment and sustainability issues – embedded
> Enterprise activities – becoming integrated across the curriculum.

The school-based Masters degree has helped retention because it is mostly undertaken by people with three to six years' experience – a group that often move out of London in search of cheaper housing. The staff development leader says:

> Individual staff have been able to apply academic skills to real situations, they have gained in confidence and they have a better understanding of wider school issues. The group has fostered good working relations between departments.

Studying while working full-time is hard, but the school helps through the:

- establishing of a group of seven people studying at the same time
- commitment of the headteacher and senior team
- sharing with staff and governors at all stages
- staff development leader's support and encouragement when necessary
- significant contribution to the MA fees by the school
- clear expectations at the outset to avoid people dropping out of the programme.

To learn more about this, watch www.teachers.tv/video/28595.

(All Teachers TV material was correct and available at the time of going to press.)

Collaborative enquiry

But you don't have to do a Masters degree course to do research. In fact the term 'research' puts some people off, which is why they talk about 'enquiry' when they try something that is closer to problem solving. For instance, perhaps case study 9.2 is more enquiry than research. Does it matter? In our eyes, the reflection, reading, thinking, trying things out and evaluation mean that research and enquiry are part of the same continuum.

Collaborative enquiry is a broader activity than school-based research or project work which is usually undertaken as an individual activity and may lead to an accredited award. It involves some staff getting together to investigate an aspect of their practice to enhance student learning. It's great if it involves sharing findings with others both within and beyond your own context. This can be a powerful motivator and is itself an effective learning process because there's a real purpose to it. Research and enquiry often snowball: one person finds that the younger boys in their class are underachieving which gets others thinking about the pupils in their class. Research raises more and more questions – and that's very exciting!

 ## Case study 9.2: Sporty naughties

What they wanted to achieve: To improve the behaviour of some disruptive pupils in Year 9.

Why? A hard core of boys in Year 9 were disrupting lessons, spoiling the learning of others and causing staff stress.

How? Staff listed and discussed the Year 9 pupils who were disrupting their lessons. The PE department was surprised as these students behaved well in sport. One of the PE teachers did some action research on sport and a strategy was devised. Staff identified 12 Year 9 'sporty naughties' defined as students who behaved in PE but were disruptive in all other subjects. They were appointed as activity leaders to organise inter-tutor group six-a-side football competitions at break time. They were responsible for the design, organisation, advertising and promotion of the activities as well as the refereeing and day-to-day running of the competitions. This involved the students talking to individual tutor groups as well as announcing fixtures and results in year group assemblies. The activity leaders were placed on monitoring cards in order to evaluate behaviour and progress in their normal lessons.

Did it work? It was very successful. Participation in the competitions was high, with large numbers of students involved, either directly in playing or in spectating. The atmosphere during break was greatly improved. The activity leaders showed improvements in their self-esteem and their behaviour in lessons was better too. The project gave strong messages about the benefit of exercise and positive behaviour strategies to other staff. The results of this project were disseminated across secondary and primary schools in the city, many of whom set up similar projects.

(From Bubb and Earley, 2008, p46)

If you want to use research and enquiry for staff development, are you or your school able to:

- commission a more knowledgeable other to be a research guide?
- help identify topics for research?
- predict what the impact will be?
- access published relevant research?
- find time for the research to happen?
- help create productive research teams?
- structure the processes and practices?
- maintain an active interest in the enquiry?
- involve pupils, parents and the community, where appropriate?
- discuss research findings with other staff?
- share research findings beyond the school?

All these are very important to create a culture where learning is seen as central to everything that is done, where there is a community of learners or a learning-centred school. Engaging in research and enquiry is a key part of such a school community and contributes to the development of a learning culture for all.

 Activity: Watch *CPD Leaders in Primary Schools – Enquiry Based Learning* www.teachers.tv/video/25620

What do you think of the way that staff engage in enquiry based learning into target-setting for writing, learning journals, developing a marking scheme with pupils and involving parents with their children's learning?

What can you learn from the way that the staff development leader facilitates the staff enquiry projects?

Coaching-mentoring

Having someone to talk to and help one reflect is a fundamental way to develop so many organisations train staff in coaching and mentoring skills. These can be used in a multitude of activities such as feedback after observations, problem solving, performance management, etc. There is, however, considerable confusion about the terms, coaching and mentoring. Mentoring is mainly about advising and helping – giving people answers. Coaching is not about giving people answers or telling them what to do but asking questions to help people find their own solutions.

Mentoring is more embedded than coaching in schools, especially for new staff but coaching is becoming more and more popular. There are different models of coaching such as STRIDE: S is for looking at people's strengths, T for identifying the target, R for what the real situation is at present, I for ideas, D for decisions and E for evaluating how well things have worked. The GROW model consists of the:

- Goal – for the session and/or project

- Reality – the current state of play

- Options – possible ways forward

- Will – commitment to planned action.

The National College has a national framework for coaching and mentoring, which has ten principles that emphasise things like how much can be learnt from conversations and that there are benefits to acting as a coach-mentor as well as being coached-mentored. It seems to be a win-win strategy but do we always give our less experienced or 'average' staff sufficient opportunities to become a coach or mentor?

CUREE has developed some interactive materials called the Effective Mentoring & Coaching suite. This contains the following titles:

- Joining up: linking coaching and mentoring with school development and performance management

- Taking hold: putting professional learners in charge of their own development through coaching

- Doubling up: securing learning and accreditation benefits from mentoring

- Letting go: developing coaches' skills in increasing professional learners' independence

- Pulling through: developing mentors' ability to support professional learners in drawing on evidence and expertise

- Pulling together: ensuring the right mix of challenge and support in co-coaching (www.curee-paccts.com).

 Activity: Watch *CPD Leaders in Primary Schools – Coaching and Mentoring* www.teachers.tv/video/25639

Consider how coaching and mentoring has improved the culture of the school workforce as well as helping individuals develop.

How could you use these examples in your setting?

In one training school with large numbers of graduate trainees, beginning teachers and NQTs, the coaching culture is so strong that hardly anyone mentions it: it has become implicit in all they do. It uses its eight ASTs to develop individuals to be better through a six week coaching programme which could include planning, modelling, observation, team teaching and discussion. Because the support is developmental even successful experienced staff request support to help them make their work even better and pupils more independent, interested and engaged.

Observation

There is a great deal of lesson observation happening in schools and colleges. This can be simply for monitoring and preparation for inspection but where it makes a difference, it's a platform for discussing specific learning and teaching. There are numerous examples of peer observation being a valuable experience when done in a mutually supportive way that encourages people to take risks. All manner of people and sessions can usefully be observed and for different lengths of time: so long as all parties know the purpose and focus. People learn a great deal from seeing different strategies used in practice but it's the dialogue that happens after the lesson where the development happens. Discussions about specific teaching and learning can boost staff and cause a snowball effect: observation and recognition breed even greater success. For more information see the chapters on observation in *Helping Teachers Develop* (Bubb, 2005) and *Successful Induction* (Bubb, 2007).

 Activity: Watch *Classroom Observation with Bayley – Questions and Answers* www.teachers.tv/video/24076

John Bayley is very skilled at discussing lessons with staff after an observation. In this film you'll see him helping others to do so. What do you think of it?

Watch *From Good to Outstanding* www.teachers.tv/video/33057

Analyse the inspector's feedback style.

Think about how you and others in your organisation feed back after an observation. What would you like to change and why?

Many schools have combined peer observation and coaching by teachers and teaching assistants. Having a framework of agreed guidelines about giving and receiving feedback, based on positivity, confidence, empowerment and clarity of action is important. The staff in one school have agreed that when giving and receiving feedback, they will:

- stick to the previously agreed focus of the observation

- listen actively to each other

- steer clear of control-oriented behaviour by avoiding mentoring and the expression of personal preferences

- frame questions to invite responses and empower colleagues

- ensure next steps are clear.

Filming can be very useful, and avoids the observer effect on pupils and staff. Some schools have observation rooms with cameras. Others film lessons for discussion in staff training. Filming a respected member of staff teaching has several benefits. The observers are seeing something really authentic, in their own setting. For the person teaching this can be celebratory – one received a heartfelt round of applause from her colleagues. She was thrilled!

Teachers TV

In our experience too few people use Teachers TV for staff development. Those who do are passionate about its benefits. There are thousands of programmes that can be watched on TV, on their website, downloaded and even edited. It's a great way of getting into other schools and colleges, picking up ideas and getting food for thought. Learning from other people's successes saves a great deal of time and can be done on a global scale. Want to know how they teach respect and manners in Japan, handwriting in France, PE in China, and sex education in Holland? There are programmes to watch from the comfort of your own computer or home.

Some staff development leaders have set up study groups with activities around programmes that deal with specific issues. This has been made easier by Teachers TV formalising this by designing materials for Teachers TV Clubs. These can have a similar format to book group meetings. Every month they supply you with four programmes and accompanying discussion questions based on a whole school issue theme like bullying, ICT skills or personalised learning. People can either watch the programmes individually or with others in your school. Then you meet as a group and discuss them using the guidance questions provided for your club. What an easy, time-saving, no cost way of getting people talking and keeping up to date with what is current in the educational world!

Reading

Reading about education and educational research is something people do little of unless they are on an accredited course: indeed our research suggests teaching assistants and other support staff seem to read more than teachers do. Perhaps one of the most individualised, cheap and flexible ways to get better at teaching and other roles in schools is through reading (or listening). And it's a lovely thing to do whether you're standing on the train going to work, sitting in the garden, lying on the sofa or even snuggled under the duvet! People use reading to get tips, ideas, food for thought and inspiration – to be better at their job. Many people have also found pearls within fiction and autobiography. Indeed, reading children's literature was the focus of a high impact project looking at helping teacher development which in turn improved pupil outcomes.

 Case study 9.3: Teachers as readers project

Phase 1 of the project funded by the Esme Fairbairn Foundation found that primary teachers' knowledge and use of children's literature in the classroom was very narrow. Phase 2 of the project focused on working with 40 primary teachers in five LAs in England for one year (2007–08) with the aim of improving their knowledge and experience of children's literature in order to help them increase pupils' motivation and enthusiasm for reading for pleasure.

The teachers' increased subject knowledge, combined with personal reflection and support enabled them to create a more inclusive reading for pleasure pedagogy. This encompassed marked improvements in reading environments, read

(Continued)

(Continued)

aloud programmes, book talk and book recommendations and the provision of quality time for independent reading. The majority of the children's attainment showed above average increases across the year. Children identified as reluctant readers became drawn into reading; their perceptions of their abilities as readers and self-confidence improved. They showed increased pleasure in reading and began to read both more regularly and more independently.

(Cremin et al., 2009)
www.ukla.org/downloads/teachers_as_readers.pdf

E-communities

Online communities are very popular and provide another easy, flexible and free form of staff development. There are many but perhaps the largest and most successful is the TES website's community at www.tes.co.uk/community. Registering is easy – the hardest part is choosing a witty username that hides your true identity. Some of the site's success must be down to the freedom that comes with this anonymity: people can ask the questions that they'd be too embarrassed to raise elsewhere. The generous sharing of resources has become formalised in the TES Resource Bank, an area where people can share materials and recommend resources and web pages.

The staffroom is freely available, 24/7 and 365 days a year. There are nearly 100 virtual corners of the staffroom where people with the same interests hang out. As well as different forums for subjects, there's a place for every type of school staff – not just teachers but trainees, admin, teaching assistants and governors as well.

There are also specialist networks. For instance, the AST network is important as the role can be quite a lonely one. Sited on the National College website www.national college.org.uk, the AST national network has six sub-sections:

1. What's new – link to AST jobs; calendar of events; forum for news; pay scales; anonymous forum and a keep up to date section with summaries of latest research, policy and other documents

2. Contact us – join the network, spreadsheet of all ASTs and an anonymous forum where you can be honest about what you love and hate about the job

3. Useful resources – for outreach, research, case studies, what works blog

4. Local Authority AST co-ordinators – spreadsheet of all LA AST co-ordinators, forum, resources, research and an anonymous forum where you can sound off or seek advice

5. Prospective ASTs – information about the assessment process, application forms, standards, pay and conditions, forum for advice

6. Specialisms – a page for each subject and aspect with a forum, links, resources.

There is much enthusiasm for the network, which is indicative of how isolated ASTs feel. They share ideas and issues. Similarly, local authority AST co-ordinators are pleased to have a way of seeing what others are doing and this improves systems because individuals aren't wasting time re-inventing the wheel.

Listening to pupils

Pupils can be a fine source of development. Ask them what they think of your work and you may be surprised at their level of sophistication. Some schools are training students to observe lessons. After observing the lesson they analyse their observations and feed back to the teacher concerned. The experience of being observed is a very rewarding one for teachers because the students give their teachers a lot of positive feedback as well as areas for development and suggestions of what to do to address these. The students are impressively knowledgeable about the learning process, about what works in the classroom and about giving effective feedback.

 Activity: Watch *Gifted and Talented Pupil Voice* www.teachers. tv/video/31897 and *Pupil Voice – Learner Teacher, Teacher Learner* www.teachers.tv/video/21718

What do you think could be the benefits of asking pupils' views?

Which staff might benefit from this form of development activity?

Role-play sessions using pupils could be a good way of demonstrating a variety of techniques for managing behaviour. It is better, of course, to select some of the naughty students who excel at drama for a really good result. Asking students to advise staff on, for instance, what 'winds them up' in the playground or the dining hall could be beneficial to staff.

Training others

Staff who plan and present training enjoy a means of development in its own right: training others, especially colleagues and peers, helps you become better at your job. In learning-centred schools, there is a culture of developing each other and benefiting from doing so. Some schools use their staff to train people in other organisations. For instance, eight teachers from a secondary school ran a bespoke middle leader development programme in a local special school. It was felt that they met the special school teachers' needs in a more effective way than a national programme such as *Leading from the Middle*. A very successful primary school in challenging circumstances, markets itself as a training provider for aspects in which it feels it has something special to share. The income earned pays for treats for pupils and staff but, as the head said, the main benefit came from the rationale that you develop by training others.

Needs should be met in the most effective way chosen from a wide menu of opportunities. Is it still the case, however, that people still equate development with going on a course? It's dangerous to get hooked into just one form or to damn another type of activity because it's out of fashion or previous experiences have not been good. The most important criterion is that it has made a difference to the person undertaking the activity so that they can do their job better. And at times a course may be what is needed. As a teacher who decided to study for a Masters degree while working full-time said:

> My main motivation for embarking on the Masters was that I wanted to learn for myself again. I had been focusing on my students' learning for a long time and felt I needed to push myself with something completely separate to my day job, but still related to the profession as a whole. (Holbrook, 2009, p11)

10

Research and resources for leaders of staff development

We've drawn upon the extensive literature on staff development – both academic and research based, practitioner orientated and from official agencies – to inform the writing of this book. In Chapter 2, under the section 'Keeping informed', we gave some websites and other sources of information to help staff development leaders keep up to date. In this chapter our focus is on published research and resources related to developing the workforce. Our selection doesn't attempt to be comprehensive but we've chosen publications which we find useful and think that you might too.

These are organised into ones about staff development leadership; the whole school workforce; support staff; and those concerning teachers' professional development. The last group is large but many of the learning points are not unique to teachers but can be applied to the wider workforce.

Useful publications

Staff development leadership

Research Into the Role of CPD Leadership in Schools

Leading and managing continuing professional development

The CPD Co-ordinator's Toolkit

Leading and co-ordinating CPD in secondary schools

Whole workforce development

The Logical Chain: CPD in Effective Schools

Staff Development Outcomes Study

Developing the Whole School Workforce: An Evaluation of the Testbed Programme

From self-evaluation to school improvement the importance of effective professional development

(Continued)

(Continued)

London's Learning

Professional learning communities

CPD impact evaluation: A guidance pack for schools

Support staff development

The Deployment and Impact of Support Staff in Schools

Exploring support staff experiences of training and development

The deployment, training and development of the wider school workforce

Teachers' professional development

GTC qualitative study of school-level strategies for teachers' CPD

Continuing professional development (CPD): the evidence base

Synthesis of research and evaluation projects concerned with capacity-building through teachers' professional development

Schools and continuing professional development (CPD) in England: State of the Nation research project

A. Staff development leadership

1. *Research Into the Role of CPD Leadership in Schools,* Robinson, M. et al., 2008, NFER, 2008

Available from: www.tda.gov.uk/upload/resources/pdf/r/research_into_cpd_leadership_in_schools.pdf

This report sets out the findings from a research study into how continuing professional development (CPD) is led in schools today, how it is supported, and the barriers and challenges faced by leaders. A large-scale postal and online survey of CPD leaders in schools was conducted in February and March 2008.

The researchers found that decision-making in CPD leadership is a complex undertaking. In primary and special schools the headteacher is most likely to make the final decision regarding opportunities for teachers and support staff, whereas in secondary schools this decision is more likely to be made by roles other than the headteacher. Overall, however, CPD leaders used methods for keeping up to date on current developments for support staff far less frequently than they did for teachers. There is a difference between forms of support currently found useful by CPD leaders and those which would be found useful. Currently the most useful forms of support for CPD leaders are conferences/workshops, and information on the provision of training and development. The support that CPD leaders would find most useful includes practical and proven methods such as toolkits for training and development, CPD leadership induction packs, and research evidence of effective practice. This may be a useful steer as to the kinds of support that could be developed and promoted further.

2. *Leading and managing continuing professional development,* Bubb, S. and Earley, P., 2007 (2nd edition), Sage

Available from: www.uk.sagepub.com/booksProdDesc.nav?contribId=528287&prodId=Book232086

The second edition of this book gives a firm knowledge base or foundation for staff development leaders, be they new to the role or experienced and wishing to think more deeply about the training and development of the school workforce. The book is made up of two parts. The first, entitled 'Professional development for school improvement', sees individual development as key to school improvement. The effective leadership of staff development is introduced through use of the development cycle (what Ofsted call the 'Logical Chain'). This cycle – of needs identification, meeting the development needs of staff, and monitoring and evaluating the impact of activities – forms the substance of Part 1, supplemented by an examination of the importance of collaborative enquiry, the sharing of practice, the growth of practitioner research and the 'research-engaged' school.

The second half of the book looks at the development of specific groups such as support staff, newly qualified teachers (NQTs), teachers in their first five years, supply teachers, middle managers, senior school leaders and governors. The issues around their roles and development needs are considered and ways suggested in which they might be met.

3. *The CPD Co-ordinator's Toolkit,* Kelly, S., 2006, Sage

Available from: www.sagepub.co.uk

This book is an easy to read resource for staff development leaders. It's rooted in the author's experience and follows her growth in understanding gained as 'a facilitator and supporter of CPD practices' in a secondary school. The book reflects the changing culture of staff development in schools and its strength lies in taking us from the basic elements of the role of co-ordinator towards the meatier issues of embedding good practice and building professional capacity across the school. There is a particularly welcome focus on the crucial role of middle and team leaders in supporting the development of members of their teams.

It includes examples of proformas, letters and PowerPoint presentations taken from the author's own practice to inform or adapt for your context. As staff development leaders you will find some really practical ideas within the proformas and PowerPoint presentations that will motivate you and save work. The author is clear that you should use these selectively and adapt for your context rather than using all the many proformas offered. It is clear from the accounts given that much of the change in practice achieved needs to be through discussion and modelling rather than paperwork.

4. *Leading and co-ordinating CPD in secondary schools, KS3 Strategy booklet and DVD,* 2005, DfES/DCSF

Available from www.dcsf.gov.uk/nationalstrategies

This booklet and DVD deserves to be read by all staff development leaders, not just the secondary ones. There is a well-written introduction that explains the key ideas in staff development and its relation to school improvement. There are ideas on supporting specific groups of teachers and an emphasis on building capacity for further professional development with sections on:

- Creating time for CPD

- Encouraging people to take responsibility for their own professional development

- Becoming a professional learning community

- Setting up teaching and learning groups

- Coaching and mentoring

- Using video to encourage reflective practice

- Developing subject knowledge

- Classroom research as CPD

- Supporting teachers at different stages in their careers

- Making the best use of leading professionals

- Evaluating the impact of CPD

- Linking CPD with performance management.

Other national strategy sources are worth consulting. These would be especially useful for trainee teachers and returners:

- *Teaching and learning in secondary schools* – 20 booklets and a DVD, on topics such as questioning, learning styles and lesson design.

- *Learning and teaching in the primary years: professional development resources* – six units with video material.

- *Professional development resource pack* – a wide range of National Literacy Strategy publications and resources.

B. Whole school workforce development

1. *The Logical Chain: CPD in Effective Schools*, 2006, Ofsted

Available from: www.ofsted.gov.uk/research/

This short report from Ofsted has been very influential. It is based primarily on visits by HMI to 29 schools (13 secondary, 14 primary and 2 special) whose inspections had identified good practice in leading and using staff development. The report describes the staff development arrangements as 'a logical chain' of procedures which entail identifying school and staff needs, planning to meet those needs, providing varied and relevant activities, involving support staff alongside teachers, monitoring progress and evaluating the impact of the professional development. This logical chain is referred to elsewhere in our book as the development cycle.

The key finding was that 'schools which had designed their CPD effectively and integrated it with their improvement plans found that teaching and learning improved and standards rose' (Ofsted, 2006, p2). Overall, staff development was found to be most effective in the schools where:

- the senior managers fully understood the connections between each link in the chain and recognised the potential of staff development for raising standards and therefore gave it a central role in planning for improvement

- all staff, enjoyed high quality development activities, which had been well chosen from a wide range of possible activities to meet their schools' and their own needs.

However, the report identified a number of concerns:

- Senior managers identified their school's needs systematically and accurately, but the identification of individual needs was not always so rigorous. Planning for the professional development of individuals was therefore often weak.

- Few schools evaluated the impact of staff development on teaching and learning successfully, largely because they failed to identify, at the planning stage, its intended outcomes and suitable evaluation methods.

- Headteachers did not know how to assess the value for money of their staff development policy.

- Well designed coaching and mentoring arrangements were highly effective in developing staff's competences, but there was wide variation in the way schools used them and, consequently, in the extent to which staff benefited from them.

- Most schools have yet to consider how the time created by workforce reform could be used for teachers' professional development.

There are some important messages in here for staff development leaders especially in terms of evaluating the impact of staff development on teaching and learning successfully.

2. *Staff Development Outcomes Study*, Bubb, S. et al., 2009, Institute of Education

Available from: www.tda.gov.uk/upload/resources/pdf/s/staff_development_outcomes_study.pdf

The main aim of the *Staff Development Outcomes Study* was to investigate how staff development, if undertaken in a systematic way across the school workforce, could lead to improved outcomes for both pupils and staff. It consisted of two phases: 35 case studies of schools (25 of them recently graded as 'outstanding' by Ofsted) and a national questionnaire survey of the school workforce.

The research found a positive association between school outcomes and staff development. The high performing case study schools mostly had strong staff development led by experienced senior staff who were well informed and devoted much time to this aspect, linking it strategically to school improvements in efficient and cost-effective ways. School ethos was fundamental to staff development. In the schools where it was strong, leaders fostered, and all staff felt, a sense of both entitlement to and responsibility for their own development and learning closely linked to benefits for the pupils. Staff turnover was low and morale was high at these schools.

There was also an association between the quality of schools' staff development and levels of pupil deprivation. Schools with low numbers of pupils entitled to free school meals were more likely to have strong staff development, more knowledgeable leaders and have more information about training opportunities than those with high numbers.

The barriers to staff development most frequently mentioned related to time, finance and support. Closure or INSET days were not being used well. Needs were met in the most effective way chosen from a wide menu of opportunities, many of which were school based. Projects and courses spanning a term or more, with activities to try out or research and involving purposeful collaboration, made most impact overall on school improvement.

3. *Developing the Whole School Workforce: An Evaluation of the Testbed Programme,* Coldwell, M. et al., 2008, Sheffield Hallam University, for the TDA.

Available from: www.tda.gov.uk/upload/resources/pdf/t/testbedsfinalreportand appendixfeb08.pdf

The Testbed project explored how schools could best facilitate the training and development of the whole school workforce. It evaluated 45 schools' approaches to whole school training and development: 15 primary, 20 secondary and 10 special schools and PRUs.

Where staff development projects were successful 'the senior leadership had a vision of, and a commitment to, whole school training and development that was reflected in school policies and supported by a strong developmental culture, in which:

- people trusted the vision and purpose of the leadership

- people were open to change

- risk-taking was accepted

- there was a general ethos of openness, participation and support

- teamwork was widely observed across the school

- motivation and morale were high' (Coldwell et al., 2008).

Interventions that gave individuals the opportunity to reflect on their own training and development led in many cases to a range of positive outcomes. In a quarter of the schools, training and development had resulted in support staff 'feeling and being regarded much more as part of the school, more equal, and more valued'. In about the same proportion there was 'evidence of impacts on general confidence/self confidence or improved self esteem for support staff working with children (almost always TAs)'. The research found that it was difficult for schools to provide evidence that their interventions were having an impact on pupils. This was due to the nature of most interventions, which had a focus on making changes to systems and staff, with expected longer term effects on pupils.

4. From self-evaluation to school improvement: the importance of effective professional development: Report for CfBT Education Trust, Bubb, S. and Earley, P. 2008, Institute of Education, for the TDA

Available from: www.cfbt.com/evidenceforeducation/pdf/Self-evaluationReport_v4(W).pdf

Taking place in the first 18 months of the requirement for schools to complete and maintain a self-evaluation form, the key research question of this study was:

> What practical steps can schools take to ensure that self-evaluation of their practice and performance leads, through the effective professional development of their staff, to genuine improvement?

The self-evaluation forms and improvement plans of 38 schools in England were analysed to track the professional development journeys that were intended to lead to planned improvement. Half of the schools were in challenging circumstances.

The report has some useful examples of schools' specific journeys from SEF to improvement – what the authors term 'Sef2Si'. Evaluating the impact of staff development was found to be the weakest link in the development cycle. In part this was because staff development was conceived conventionally in terms of activities to be engaged in (inputs) rather than as the actual development of professional knowledge and expertise (outcomes). The question 'what will happen as a result of this staff development activity' was rarely asked. The report argues that staff development is not definable as a course, a programme of training or study, or even as a set of learning experiences. Rather, adult learning is the outcome that may result from any or all of these staff development activities and from the individual's reflection on day-to-day experience of doing the job.

5. London's Learning, 2007

Available from: www.cpd.lgfl.net

This resource was started by practitioners for practitioners in 2005 as a result of a development project building on the thinking of a group of people with responsibility for leading staff development. Materials are organised within seven key principles which underpin the development of a learning-centred community:

- Leadership of CPD

- High quality opportunities for CPD

- CPD, school improvement and performance management

- CDP for all staff

- Working in partnership

- Resources

- Evaluation of impact.

The first principle, 'Leadership of CPD', emphasises that the role is about creating a vision, culture, and strategy for CPD. To ensure the resource would offer support for all staff development leaders, participants described their practice in leading professional development in three stages: emerging, developing and establishing.

The resource can be used in various ways such as to structure network meetings for staff development leaders around one of the seven principles as a springboard to share practice.

6. *Professional learning communities: source materials for school leaders and other leaders of professional learning*, Stoll, L., et al., 2006. DfES, NCSL and GTC

Available from: www.nationalcollege.org.uk

This resource is derived from the findings of Bolam et al.'s (2006) research study *Creating and sustaining effective professional learning communities*, DCSF RR637 (www.dcsf.gov.uk/research/data/uploadfiles/RR637.pdf). The researchers define a professional learning community (PLC) as 'an inclusive group of people, motivated by a shared learning vision, who support and work with each other, finding ways, inside and out-side, their immediate community, to enquire on their practice and together learn new and better approaches that will enhance all pupils' learning'. However, becoming a PLC is hard because it requires changing the culture, which is where the pack comes in handy. It contains a sheet explaining what PLCs are, a user guide, and a route map to assist in planning your journey through the 13 booklets. After some activities that help deepen understanding about PLCs, these materials give step by step suggestions of how to audit your organisation, plan how you want it to develop, ideas for action, and lastly how to monitor and evaluate the impact of your PLC.

There are a range of different activities such as reading short articles, auditing current practice and sorting quotations into different characteristics of PLCs. Identifying your present school culture is a sensible place to start and these materials suggest fun ways to do so such as looking at what messages the entrance area conveys, asking pupils to take photos, and getting staff to think of metaphors for what their learning community is like. How about a lava lamp with different blobs of oil rising and falling?

There's much to draw on in this pack for professional development sessions using self-evaluation, reflective enquiry, dialogue, collaborative learning and problem solving. Its pitch is refreshingly intellectual as well as practical: activities like the group discussion on readings from four publications would support colleagues working on a Masters course. All in all, this pack offers an accessible, well thought through path of activities for staff development leaders.

7. *Workfoce Development Needs Analysis Pack,* Lincoln: Lincolnshire School Improvement Service CfBT

Available from: www.cpdleader.com

The TDA's e-directory identifies a number of toolkits and packs that have been developed by groups of local authorities including this one produced by the East Midlands consortium. This particular pack has been included because it considers the problematic area of CPD impact evaluation and it builds upon the government-funded research study *Evaluating the impact of CPD* (Goodall et al., 2005). CfBT Lincolnshire School Improvement Service worked with the research team and a number of schools to develop guidance materials on aspects of CPD monitoring and evaluation. Goodall et al's *Route Map and Tool Kit for the Evaluation of the Impact of Continuing Professional Development in Schools* (DfES, 2005) formed the basis of this work. The guidance supplements are in the East Midlands CPD toolkit available to schools across the nine East Midlands authorities, accessible electronically on the Resources and Materials database part of the Lincolnshire School Improvement Service website and on www.cpd leader.com.

This pack includes sections entitled:

- The key principles of effective CPD evaluation
- CPD impact: pitfalls to avoid
- What does the research say about CPD impact evaluation?
- CPD impact: the 4 key dimensions
- A CPD monitoring and evaluation strategy
- CPD impact: using the pupil voice
- CPD impact: possible success criteria
- 'Value for money': measuring the benefits of different types of workforce development
- Effective dissemination
- How good is CPD in our school?

The last section on how good is CPD in your school is particularly useful and provides a checklist which can be used for auditing purposes. It provides brief descriptions defining the key characteristics of staff development under the headings of outstanding, good, satisfactory and inadequate. It can be used in conjunction with school self-evaluation systems to assess the current quality and to consider some of the requirements for improvement.

The *Workforce development needs analysis* has case studies and a wealth of useful material.

C. Support staff development

1. *The Deployment and Impact of Support Staff in Schools*, Blatchford, P. et al., 2007, RR005, DCSF

Available from: www.dcsf.gov.uk/research/data/uploadfiles/DCSF-RR005.pdf

The number and range of support staff working in schools has increased considerably over the last decade but there is still a shortage of research into this part of the school workforce. Blatchford et al.'s longitudinal study, funded by the DCSF, is one of the few that have looked at the deployment of support staff in schools. Based on a large-scale postal survey of schools, support staff and teachers in 2006, they found, for example:

- Only 10 per cent of support staff had no qualifications and over a third (38 per cent) had qualifications above GCSE level. Site staff, along with other pupil support and especially facilities staff, had the lowest qualifications.

- In comparison to the earlier survey, support staff were now significantly more likely to be provided with a job description, and to have been appraised over the last year.

- There was little sign that attendance at training had increased over the past two years.

- The majority of teachers (75 per cent) had not been trained to work with support staff, either in the classroom or as line managers.

- The majority of teachers did not have allocated planning or feedback time with support staff.

This research provides some interesting food for thought and will enable you to compare your own practice with the national picture.

2. *Exploring support staff experiences of training and development*, Teeman, D. et al., 2008, NFER/Ipsos MORI, TDA

Available from: www.tda.gov.uk/upload/resources/pdf/s/sss_gf.pdf

The study's main purpose is to explore support staff perceptions and experiences of training and development over a three-year period (June 2006 to May 2009). This report presents the findings from the first survey, conducted in the autumn term of 2006, and it provides a 'baseline' to measure any changes over time.

Three-fifths of support staff said they felt 'very well supported' and around a third 'fairly well supported'. Very few (under one in ten) said that they did not feel supported by their school. However, whilst the majority (75 per cent) had received some form of professional development in the 12 months preceding the survey, a quarter (24 per cent) had not. Those who said they did not have a formal/ written contract, staff aged 55 and over, and those working part-time were most likely not to have had training and development. The majority of support staff agreed that they would prefer training and development to be held 'at or near' their own school.

Over two-thirds of respondents said the training and development they received had helped support them in carrying out their role. One in seven felt they had gained confidence but one in 20 said that there had been no benefits. Two-thirds of support staff identified a range of factors which they said prevented them from taking part in training and development. Just under a third of support staff said that other commitments and demands on their time prevented them from taking part in training and development. Lack of funding was also identified as a barrier by one in seven of support staff. A fifth of support staff respondents did not know where to obtain information about training and development.

3. *The deployment, training and development of the wider school workforce*, 2008, Ofsted

Available from: www.ofsted.gov.uk/research

This is the fourth report by Ofsted on the effectiveness of the reforms to the school workforce. It shows that, compared with the findings of earlier surveys, schools are using more reliable indicators to monitor and assess the effectiveness of workforce reform. Members of the wider workforce are particularly successful in engaging pupils at risk of underachievement or permanent exclusion, in developing links with the community and in increasing the involvement of parents and carers in their children's learning. Schools are at very different stages of managing and developing the wider workforce, with few providing a coherent cycle of induction and training, performance management and career development.

D. Teacher development

GTC qualitative study of school-level strategies for teachers' CPD, CUREE, Cordingley, P., 2008

Available from: www.gtce.org.uk/research

This research looks at the important area of strategic teacher development. It addresses several questions, including:

- What is a good and consensual working definition of 'strategic' CPD?

- What are the barriers to a more strategic approach being developed?

- Where strategic approaches are judged to be in place, what range of CPD concepts and opportunities are deployed in support of this?

- How is CPD evaluated and its impact assessed at a strategic level?

- What appear to be the key managerial and operational characteristics of a strategic approach and what are the benefits?

The report looks in detail at four named schools (a primary, special and two secondaries) where leaders are thinking and acting strategically when it comes to staff development planning and implementation. Although the strategic development of teachers is the focus of the research there is much that is transferable to the whole school workforce.

2. *Continuing professional development (CPD): the evidence base,* CUREE, Cordingley, P., et al., 2008

Avaliable from: www.tda.gov.uk/upload/resources/pdf/e/eppi_research.pdf

This summary presents the cumulative evidence from four systematic reviews of research about effective staff development. The key messages are that CPD that was linked to positive benefits usually involved the following:

- peer support (in pairs or small groups) to encourage, extend and structure professional learning, dialogue and experimentation – *in combination with*

- specialist support, including modelling, workshops, observation, feedback, coaching – a menu of research-based strategies for enhancing learning

- planned meetings for structured discussion – including exploring evidence from the teachers' classrooms about their experiments with new approaches and of their beliefs about teaching, their subjects and their learners

- processes for sustaining the CPD over time to enable teachers to embed the practices in their own classroom settings – including informal day-to-day discussions and observations between teachers, and using work they would have to do anyway (such as lesson planning and designing schemes of work or curriculum development) as a springboard for learning in workshops

- recognition and analysis of teachers' individual starting points and building on what they know and can do already

- developing teachers' ownership of their learning by offering scope to identify or refine their own learning focus (within a menu set by the programme or the school), and the opportunity to take on a degree of leadership in their CPD, and

- a focus on pupil learning and pupil outcomes, often as a way to analyse starting points, structure development discussions and evaluate progress, both formatively and summatively.

The most effective type of development activity, which was clearly linked to the strongest or widest ranging positive effects for staff and pupils, was found to be collaborative. That is, the facilitators and designers of the activity planned to involve two or more people working together on a sustained basis to experiment with new practice, as a specific learning strategy.

3. Synthesis of research and evaluation projects concerned with capacity-building through teachers' professional development, Bolam, R. and Weindling, D., 2006, GTCE

Available from: www.gtce.org.uk/research

This review, commissioned by the General Teaching Council (England) and the ATL synthesises the findings from 20 studies of teachers' professional development in England. There was evidence about the importance of the roles of heads and senior staff; including support staff with teachers in staff development and other aspects of professional learning communities; and school culture in the improvement of staff development. More specifically, there was strong evidence which showed that staff development was important in promoting research engagement and a professional learning community within the school. They found that:

- the more influence teachers had over their own staff development the more likely they were to consider it effective

- the majority of teachers equated staff development with a traditional view of in-service training. There was also fairly strong evidence that for staff development to be effective it needed to be delivered in much broader courses than short training sessions

- effective staff development had a positive impact on pupil learning

- the role of the staff development leader is important.

The authors consider the research studies' findings and how they might contribute to the policy on staff development for capacity building in schools.

4. Schools and continuing professional development (CPD) in England: State of the Nation research project, Synthesis report, Pedder, D. et al., 2008, TDA

Available from: www.tda.gov.uk/upload/resources/pdf/t/SoNfinalreport.pdf

The TDA commissioned *State of the Nation* research concluded that more attention should be paid to teacher personal development and well-being in an educational climate of escalating performance demands. The research found that the organisation of CPD tended not to be strategic and teachers' professional development needs were rarely addressed. CPD outcomes were seen as very fragmented and ad hoc and there was no expectation that discussion about this would be part of the performance management process.

The survey found that teachers participated in a wide range of development activities, but gaining accreditation was not important to them. School leaders perceived that school-based activities provided better value for money than external events, so for example in-school workshops, mentoring and teacher networks were rated highly and accredited courses lowly. Secondary schools spent far more on external courses than primary schools. The researchers found that training had little impact beyond the individuals involved despite teachers generally reporting a significant amount of sharing of learning from CPD activities. This was because activities were not sustained, continuous or embedded over time.

In two-thirds of the State of the Nation research schools the emerging view was that there were no insurmountable or significant barriers to accessing CPD, however, custom and practice understandings of budgets and time available resulted in self-regulation by teachers and a strong sense of what it was 'reasonable' to request in this area of school life.

References

Atherton, A. (2005) 'Visits to other schools – the "February 11th project"', *Professional Development Today*, 8(3): 20–25.

Blatchford, P., Bassett, P., Brown, P., Martin, C., Russell, B. and Webster, A. (2007) *The Deployment and Impact of Support Staff in Schools*, RR005, London: DCSF.

Bolam, R., McMahon, A., Stoll, L., Thomas S., Wallace, M., Greenwood, A. and Hawkey, K. (2006) *Creating and Sustaining Effective Professional Learning Communities*, London: DfES.

Bolam, R. and Weindling, D. (2006) *Synthesis of research and evaluation projects concerned with capacity-building through teachers' professional development*. Available from: www.gtce.org.uk/research/commissioned_res/cpd1/

British Market Research Bureau (BMRB) (2008) *Teachers' Workload Diaries – March 2008*, London: HMSO.

Bubb, S. (2005) *Helping Teachers Develop*, London: Sage.

Bubb, S. (2007) *Successful Induction*, London: Sage.

Bubb, S. and Earley, P. (2007) *Leading and managing continuing professional development* (2nd edition), London: Sage.

Bubb, S. and Earley, P. (2008) *From self-evaluation to school improvement: the importance of effective staff development*, Reading: CfBT research report.

Bubb, S., Earley, P. and Hempel-Jorgensen, A. (2009) *Staff Development Outcomes Study*, London: Institute of Education.

CfBT/Lincs SIP (2007) *Workforce Development Needs Analysis Pack*, Lincoln: Lincs School Improvement Service/CfBT.

Coldwell, M., Simkins, T., Coldron, J. and Smith, R. (2008) *Developing the Whole School Workforce: An Evaluation of the Testbed Programme*, London: TDA.

Cordingley, P. (2008a) *GTC qualitative study of school-level strategies for teachers' CPD: Report by CUREE*. Available from: www.gtce.org.uk/research/commissioned_res/cpd1/

Cordingley, P. (2008b) *Sauce for the Goose: Learning entitlements that work for teachers as well as for their pupils*, Coventry: CUREE.

Cordingley, P. and Temperley, J. (2006) *Leading Continuing Professional Development in School Networks: Adding Value, Securing Impact*, Coventry: CUREE.

Cremin, T., Mottram, M., Collins, F., Powell, S. and Safford, K. (2009) *Teachers as readers: building communities of practice. Executive summary*. Available from: www.ukla.org/downloads/teachers_as_readers.pdf

Davies, B. and Davies, B. (2009) 'Strategic Leadership', in Davies, B. (ed) *The Essentials of School Leadership*. London: Sage.

Day, C. (2008) 'A career's worth of CPD', *CPD Update*, July. Last accessed 16 April 2009, www.teachingexpertise.com/articles/careers-worth-cpd-4052

Day, C., Stobard, G., Sammons, P., Kington, A., Gu, Q., Smees, R. and Mujaba, T. (2006) *Variations in Teachers' Work, Lives and Effectiveness (VITAE)*, London: DCSF.

Dennison, B. and Kirk, R. (1990) *Do, Review, Learn, Apply: A Simple Guide to Experiential Learning*, Oxford: Blackwell.

Department for Children, Schools and Families (DCSF) (2008) *School Teachers' Pay and Conditions Document*, London: DCSF.

Department for Education and Skills (DfES) (2006) *Families of Schools*, London: DfES.

Department for Education and Skills (DfES) and Department for Children, Schools and Families (DCSF) (2005) Leading and co-ordinating CPD in secondary schools, KS3 Strategy booklet and DVD, London: DfES/DCSF.

Department of Education and Science (DES) (1972) *The James Report: Teacher Education and Training.* London: HMSO.

Edgar, B. (2009) 'We deserve better team meetings!', *Professional Development Today*, 12(1): 39–45.

Earley, P. and Porritt, V. (eds) (2009) *Effective Practice in Continuing Professional Development: Lessons from Schools*, London: Institute of Education and TDA, Bedford Way series.

Frost, D. and Durrant, J. (2003) *Teacher-led Development Work*, London: David Fulton.

Glaser, R. (2002) *Designing and Facilitating Adult Learning*, King of Prussia, PA: HRDQ.

Goodall, J., Day, C., Harris, A., Lindsey, G. and Muijs, D. (2005) *Evaluating the impact of continuing professional development*, Nottingham: DCSF. http://dcsf.gov.uk/rsgateway

Guskey, T. (2002) 'Does it make a difference? Evaluating professional development', *Educational Leadership*, March: 45–51.

Guskey, T. (2005) 'A Conversation with Thomas R. Guskey', *The Evaluation Exchange*, 11(4): 12–15.

Holbrook, C. (2009) 'The master class', *Professional Teacher*, Spring, London: TDA.

Izzett, T. (2009) 'Planning my non-contact time is equally as valuable as lesson planning', *Professional Teacher*, Spring, London: TDA.

Joyce, B.R. and Showers, B. (2002) *Student Achievement through Staff Development* (3rd edition), VA, USA: Association for Supervision and Curriculum Development.

Kelly, S. (2006) *The CPD Co-ordinator's Toolkit*, London: Sage.

London's Learning (2007) Available from: www.cpd.lgfl.net

Margo, J., Benton, M., Withers, K. and Sodha, S. (2008) *Those Who Can*, London: IPPR.

McCormick, R., Banks, F., Morgan, B., Opfer, D., Pedder, D., Storey, A. and Wolfenden, F. (2008) *Schools and Continuing Professional Development in England – State of the Nation Research Project*, London: TDA.

National Foundation for Educational Research (NFER) (2008) *Teacher Voice Omnibus Surveys*, Slough: NFER.

Office for Standards in Education (Ofsted) (2006) *The Logical Chain*, London: Ofsted.

Office for Standards in Education (Ofsted) (2008) *The deployment, training and development of the wider school workforce*, London: Ofsted.

Pedder, D., Storey, A. and Opfer, D. (2008) *Schools and continuing professional development (CPD) in England: State of the Nation research project, Synthesis report*, London: TDA.

Porritt, V. (2008) 'What's in a name?', *INSTEAD*, 4, London: Institute of Education.

Robinson, M., Walker, M., Kinder, K. and Haines, B. (2008) *Research Into the Role of CPD Leadership in Schools*, Slough: NFER.

South Yorkshire LEAs (2006) *CPD Tool Kit*.

Speck, M. and Knipe, C. (2005) *Why can't we get it right?: Professional development in our schools*, London: Sage.

Stoll, L., Bolam, R., McMahon, A., Thomas, S., Wallace, M., Greenwood, A. and Hawkey, K. (2006) *Professional learning communities: source materials for school leaders and other leaders of professional learning*, London: DfES, NCSL and GTC.

Storey, A., Banks, F., Cooper. D., Cunningham, P., Ebbutt, D., Fox, A., Morgan, B., Pedder, D. and Wolfenden, F. (2008) *Schools and Continuing Professional Development (CPD) in England – State of the Nation Research Project.* London: TDA.

Teeman, D., Walker, M. and Sharp, C. (2008) *Exploring Support Staff Experiences of Training and Development*, NFER/Ipsos MORI, London: TDA.

Weindling, D. and Earley, P. (1987) *Secondary Headship: the first years.* Windsor: NfER Nelson.

Author Index

Subject Index